MW00617759

PERSONAL GROWTH TO POWER

Jesus Between the Lines

By

Dr. C. Thomas Anderson

18 Power Principles to Success

If Followed, Success Cannot Elude You

Copyright © 2016 The Word For Winners

Printed in the United States of America. All rights reserved under International Copyright Law. Contents and/or cover may not be reproduced in whole or in part in any form without the express written consent of The Word For Winners©

FIRST EDITION

The Word For Winners©
P.O. Box 22229
Mesa, AZ 85215
thewordforwinners.com

ISBN: 9781682734629

PERSONAL GROWTH TO POWER
Jesus Between the Lines
18 Power Principles to Success
If Followed, Success Cannot Elude You

Dr. C. Thomas Anderson
Drcthomasanderson.org

Janice Marie Grant - Publishing Editor / Layout
Dana Hedden - Editor
Susan Gross - Co-Editor

PERSONAL GROWTH TO POWER
Jesus Between The Lines

18 Power Principles to Success
If Followed, Success Cannot Elude You

Table of Contents

Table of Contents Continued

Table of Contents Continued

Critical Thoughts

Thought I

Power that steals freedom of choice and responsibility for life is wrong use of power. Power that brings life, light, accountability and love is God's plan and produces the right product!

Thought II

Money creates power, but understanding right use of power can create wealth.

Thought III

Our purpose on earth is to be fruitful, multiply, fill the earth, have dominion and authority, which is power. Natural power and spiritual power are crucial to success.

Revelation 1:5-6 (NKJ)

[5] *...Jesus Christ...* [6] *has made us kings and priests...giving us natural authority and supernatural authority.*

Matthew 7:24-27 (NIV)

[24]*Therefore everyone who hears these words of mine and puts them into practice is like a wise man who built his house on the rock.*

[25]*The rain came down, the streams rose, and the winds blew and beat against that house; yet it did not fall, because it had its foundation on the rock.*

²⁶*But everyone who hears these words of mine and does not put them into practice is like a foolish man who built his house on sand.*

²⁷*The rain came down, the streams rose, and the winds blew and beat against that house, and it fell with a great crash.*

Personal Power Principles

The following Personal Power Principles were all found by following Christ's life on earth as written in the Gospels. These Power Principles can be misused and misunderstood by some.

If they are followed and applied with a right heart, right attitude, and for the right reasons, (to further the kingdom of God and produce success for you on earth) you will enjoy a glorious outcome by studying and applying them.

ONE OF THE BEST PARTS OF
THE ENTIRE BOOK!

Introduction
Personal Growth to Power
If Followed, Success Cannot Elude You

Important Thoughts

Not every thought is an important one. We often have foolish thoughts, wrong thoughts, judgmental thoughts, condescending thoughts. All kinds of thoughts, from a variety of sources, enter our head. We think up thoughts ourselves, we get thoughts from outside influences. Our thoughts, wherever they come from, are influential. What we think about and dwell upon form our beliefs, which in turn determines how we act or react.

Below are thoughts I consider necessary for a successful life. Understanding and meditating on these thoughts will make your life better.

- Desire is more important than intelligence.

- Meditating on what we desire produces passion.

- Principles are more important than knowledge.

- Focused thought produces attitude.

- The best way to manage the future is to create it.

- All power comes from God, through the creation for the creation.

4

Thoughts become ideas. Meditating on an idea creates desire for that idea. Additional, detailed meditation increases passion for that idea. It can be positive or negative passion depending on the thought. Meditating on the important thoughts listed above will produce positive passion for positive principles. This passion will produce attitudes of the heart resulting in the actions and behaviors necessary to successfully persevere and accomplish an idea to its end.

An idea is a vision. A vision without action is just a hallucination. Action without vision is merely random activity. It is passion for an idea that fuels the action. Passion acted upon in faith will develop actions that produce desired results. Meditate on positive, encouraging thoughts like the ones listed previously. They will help you achieve your vision.

Knowledge and intelligence may get you a job, but the passion and principles you demonstrate while doing that job will determine whether or not you keep the job and how good you become at the job.

What you believe, your belief system, is the result of what thoughts you allow into your subconscience, or heart. Where you are today is a direct result of your thoughts, desires, passions, attitudes and beliefs - your principles. These principles of your heart-thoughts have brought you to your current destination. Are you where you want to be?

Personal Power Principle 1
Walking, Talking, Living Soul
The Walk, The Talk, The Dress

Your dress, walk, talk, and confidence can cause you to stand out in a crowd. Be intentional; create a first impression of power, strength and confidence that draws.

Jesus walked the earth with just such a presence. People noticed Him and wanted to get to know Him. When I think about this phenomenon, a Carly Simon song pops into my mind;

"You walked into the party like you were walking onto a yacht. Your hat strategically dipped below one eye, your scarf, it was apricot... You're so vain you probably think this song is about you..."

The songwriter noticed the person's walk, the hat, the scarf and a perceived attitude of this person walking into the party. She made a judgment call based on what she saw, vanity. Our appearance and demeanor say things about us. True or not, people make decisions about who and how we are within the first few seconds. We all have different kinds of mentalities and attitudes which make up our belief system. Jesus' belief system gave Him an air of peaceful confidence. Wherever He went, people wanted to know Him and get close to Him.

Consider the story of Jesus' baptism. After being baptized, He was taken immediately into the desert. For forty days He slept on a rock, was hauled all over the place, or if you will, allowed Himself to be hauled all over the place by the enemy. After defeating the enemy with the Word of God, Jesus showed up at the Sea of Galilee. Thinking about this story, you may immediately have certain thoughts, mental pictures, and attitudes about how He looked after being in the desert for forty days. Was He a mess? Maybe pushing a shopping cart and collecting aluminum cans? If that was accurate, *"Come follow Me"* would not have been successfully received by anyone. Jesus' words, however, were persuasive and met with agreement. The disciples looked at Him and knew instantly He was a person worth following.

Like attracts like, rich follow rich, poor follow poor. Rich do not follow poor. The Bible gives a simple account of Jesus as He walked by the Sea of Galilee. It doesn't indicate He stopped. It says He walked by and said, *"Come, follow me; I'll make you fishers of men,"* and people followed.

There had to be something about His walk, something about His look, something about His voice, something about Him! The men who followed were successful businessmen who owned their own businesses. They hired others to help them work. But when Jesus called, they immediately dropped their nets and said, "I'm with You." There was something very special about Jesus.

Now, religion might say there was an 'aura of God' about Him. I don't believe that was the case. At that time He was 100% man. Just like you or I, Jesus walked the earth as a human being. He was filled with the Spirit, yes, but He was a man. He was tempted in every way, just as we are tempted. It was necessary for Him to be 100% human so He could overcome every sin on the earth, nail it to the cross and set all humanity free. He walked the earth as a man; consequently, whatever He had going for Him, we can have it too.

What was it about Jesus that made Him so convincing? What did He have going for Him that caused people to drop everything in their life and follow Him without question? They didn't stop to get their business in order, pack their bags, or get Traveler's Cheques. They just got up from wherever they were, stopped whatever they were doing and followed Him. I believe

His power was in His walk, His talk, His dress and how He carried Himself. A sense of confidence came from Jesus that was pretty dramatic. He obtained the same positive results with the twelve disciples.

So let's think about what He was like. He stood out, He was conspicuous. There must have been hundreds of people who walked where He did at the same time He did. Everyone noticed Him. He did not blend in with the bland, timid masses.

There is an interesting dynamic going on in the world today. Watch a group of teenagers. They all want to dress alike, have the same hair cut, and use the same slang. They have adopted a "blend-in" mentality. Each one will tell you they are being an individual, but the truth is they all look alike and are doing the same thing. Too many people today have become homogenized, adopted status quo.

If someone with confidence or someone who is accomplished enters the room, people notice because they don't blend in. People are drawn to that person. Everyone wants to know that person. There is something to this phenomenon. Science has discovered that our communication is 55% non-verbal. The actual words we use are only 7% of our communication. The tonality of those words, the volume, the inflection, the speed, etc., comprises 38% of our communication. Body language is a powerful communicator.

Like any skill, communication is something we learn. You can train yourself to be more aware of your communication. Be intentional in your verbal and non-verbal communication cues. Work at improving. Set a reasonable improvement goal, perhaps ten percent, in a reasonable time period. There are immediate improvements you can make. Wear clothes that are clean and pressed. Make certain your shoes are cleaned and/or shined. Get a hair cut if needed. Always have clean hair styled appropriately. A Mohawk may be a cool haircut, but it might not give the impression you're seeking.

Make eye contact when you are speaking to someone. Give a firm hand shake. Speak clearly, enunciate your words. Walk tall, back straight, head held high. Smile! People are affected by your facial attitude. You can exude confidence by incorporating these things into your life. Walk as though you own the place, not in pride, but as a representative of the King of Kings.

I work at looking sharp, at standing out. My white hair helps. I have had it since I was seventeen. You can imagine how much it made me stand-out back then. I didn't appreciate my white hair till I was older. But I always dress in clean, pressed clothes. My shoes are always shined. I intentionally look my best at all times.

Confidence in your voice is also a powerful tool. Take time to practice speaking. Elvis used to sing in front of a mirror a half hour before each performance to build his confidence. He was terrified of crowds. Confidence can be practiced and learned, but the best confidence we can have is in knowing who we are in Christ Jesus. Our confidence comes through Him, not a mirror.

Be confident when you speak, but also let people know that you care about them. Having a heart of genuine care and concern can open many doors. Our confidence and compassion comes from Jesus. We represent Him wherever we go. We are ambassadors of Christ, the King of Kings. How we look and act reflects directly on Him. His love showing through us (as we realize who we are in Him) materializes as confidence.

Another part of confidence is knowledge. I don't mean go back to college and get a master's degree, although that might be a step for some. Be able to converse on a variety of subjects.

Too often we focus on our job, our family, our home and nothing else. These are all important, but there is more to life than just that small circle. Do you work your 40 or 60 hour week, then go home and zone out on the television. What do you watch? Is it educational or personally uplifting? I am not crazy about news because it is so negative, but I want to know what is going on so I can talk intelligently with people. I don't want to be naïve about the world around me.

When you develop knowledge, you gain confidence. Your vision becomes clearer and you are able to explore and explain more details of your vision. A clear vision enables stronger meditation which increases passion that translates into action toward manifesting your vision. Additionally, increased knowledge draws people to you. We can't be a Christian witness if we don't draw people to us.

Increased knowledge is a powerful tool. Reading books is another excellent way to increase your knowledge and your vocabulary. I try to read a book a week, but not everyone is able to read that quickly. Challenge yourself to read at least one book a month. And I am not talking about fiction novels that just fill your head with illusions. I am talking about personal growth books. If it doesn't help you in some way, why read the book? Learn a new word each week, spelling and definition. Try to use that word at least one time a day each day of that week.

When you adopt an attitude of learning, you will be amazed at how quickly you accumulate information and knowledge. And it's fun! As soon as you gain some knowledge, you want to tell someone else. When you share it with someone, you make a deeper mental imprint. You remember the information because you have increased the amount of electric chemicals in your brain and built new pathways. The new knowledge is now stored energy.

Assimilating knowledge is just part of learning and growing. When knowledge becomes understanding, understanding produces wisdom of life. Life is no accident; we were beautifully and wonderfully made. Learn and grow. Become the person you were always intended to be.

HOW DO I...

Dress? _____

_____

Walk? _____

_____

Talk? _____

_____

WHAT...

Knowledge Do I have? _____

_____

Do I Desire to Change? _____

_____

Steps Will I Take? _____

_____

AND...

How Committed Am I? _____

_____

Personal Power Principle 2
Get Lucky
Hang With God

Avoid negative energy people. They take power from you to fill their own void. Hang out with the blessed and happy people; you are influenced by your associates! Be responsible for who you are and who you will become. Jesus loved all people but His inner circle consisted of grounded, positive people.

I realize this may draw criticism. It doesn't sound Christian; however, it is exactly what Jesus did. This principle, as are all the Personal Power Principles, comes directly from the Word of God. Jesus did hang out with people of intelligence and wealth. It may be a little difficult for us to grasp, but there is a reason why He chose His close associates from this group of people.

Jesus walked past many sick, poor, and miserable people on His way into Jericho. He did not ask to stay with any of them. He chose Zacchaeus, a tax collector (Luke 19). He didn't ask Zacchaeus if he had a house, so we can assume that his dress and demeanor spoke of his wealth. The Bible does say that Zacchaeus was the chief tax collector, a very wealthy man. So Jesus went to the home of a wealthy, unbelieving sinner to spend the day. Many eyebrows were raised by this decision. Jesus was called a wine bibber and a glutton because He stayed with people of wealth who had the means to provide an abundance of food and wine.

The twelve disciples were wealthy men. Now, unfortunately, if today's church needed twelve men, they would go down to the unemployment office, choose men for the job to help out the poor and boost the economy. The effect, though, would only be on a very small scale. Jesus went out and found twelve businessmen. They were successful, they had money, they were working, and they followed Him without losing anything. Case in point, after Jesus was arrested, Peter went back to his boat and resumed fishing.

Why did he choose men of current success to join His ministry? This principle is popular in the business world today, using a multi-level strategy or synergy. Take twelve successful, intelligent people who each go out and touch twelve more that will touch twelve more. The sum total of those two levels of encounter by themselves equal 1,728 people. And we know that hundreds were touched by each disciple and each person they touched went on to touch many others, not just one. If Jesus had chosen twelve needy men, much time would have been used to teach them the principles of success, bring them out of a poverty mentality, and for them to gain the financial means to travel the world and touch others with the Good News.

This is not to say that everyone who is poor has a victim mentality or everyone who is not a successful business person is incapable of sharing the Good News, absolutely not. Jesus chose the disciples because He had a short time here on the earth and He had much to accomplish. He needed to maximize His efforts in the time allotted. He chose those who were the best investment for the time and purpose at hand.

Jesus hung out with individuals who could afford the best. Jesus, too, was wealthy. The three wise men brought gifts of gold, frankincense and myrrh when He was born, He had more than enough. Too often Jesus is characterized as poor from the statement recorded in Matthew and Luke, "Foxes have holes and birds of the air have nests, but the Son of Man has nowhere to lay His head." This is an Aramaic idiom meaning "you cannot go where I am going." Mysteries are hidden in the Word of God for us, not from us. We have a responsibility to study and understand God's Word. He gave it for our benefit so we could grow and be accountable.

Jesus loved every single person, regardless of social status or wealth. He healed the poor and the rich; He laid down His life for all. He was particular, however, about who He allowed to be in His inner circle. Why? The Law of Attraction: like pulls like. We are what we think, not what we think we are (*As he thinks in his heart, so is he...* Proverbs 27:3). Everything is made of energy. When we think, we send out energy vibrations. Technology is available to measure the electrical current created by our thoughts.

Think about how a radio works. A transmitter sends out energy waves which are picked up by a radio (the receiver) when it is tuned to the proper wavelength. Likewise, we are always sending out electrical vibrations from our brain in the form of energy thought waves. Those around us pick up the waves and are affected by them whether they know it or not. When we are around negative people, we become negative. When we associate with people who are thinking, resourceful, and cheerful; we become thoughtful, resourceful, and cheerful. This is why it is important to surround ourselves with people who broadcast the kind of energy we wish to emulate. It is why Jesus chose successful people to be His inner circle, His disciples.

We are responsible for our own well-being, physically, mentally, emotionally and spiritually. We cannot blame others for how we are or what we do. Although we cannot control all of the things that happen, the circumstances or the situations that occur around us, we can control how we react to those circumstances and situations. We have the God-given gift of choice. We choose, intentionally or unintentionally. Not choosing is a choice. We reap what we sow mentally, physically, emotionally and spiritually. Jesus told us in John 10:10, *"I have come that*

they may have life, and that they may have it more abundantly."
People who stay in a negative energy state do not believe abundance is for them. They do not believe they can change. They lack faith. They choose not to believe.

The woman with the twelve-year issue of blood chose to believe and was healed when she touched Jesus' garment. He told her to *"go and be healed,"* that *"her faith"* had made her whole (Matthew 9:20). Jesus made her responsible and accountable for her life when He told her to go and be healed. He had helped her, now it was time for her to help herself. Another example is the demoniac at Gadarenes (Luke 8:26-39). After all the demons left him, the man requested to go with Jesus. He was told to go back to town and make amends for what he had done to the town's people while he was 'under the influence'. Jesus made him responsible for his actions. The man was cured spiritually, but he still had work to do on himself. He had mental and emotional issues which needed healing. Jesus made him accountable for this part. He did not allow victims to become involved in His life. He had a ministry to build, something to do for God. So He surrounded Himself with people who gave positive energy. Likewise, we should hang with positive people who make positive choices, not those who suck the life out of us.

There are people who will attach themselves to your life and suck you dry of your life's blood. They will come to you and say, "You're the only one that can help me. You're the only one who cares. Won't you help me? Won't you help me?" Of course, good-intentioned Christians go, "Oh, yes, how can I help?" That loving Christian is or becomes just as dysfunctional as the victim. They get their worth from keeping someone sick instead of helping make them well. They invest their time, their money, and their resources, and do things that are not building or teaching. Then one day, the do-gooder will run out of strength, time, money, patience or all the above. They'll be tired of helping, drained of all of their energy, and will finally say, "Enough!" And, of course, the person they have been helping will turn on them viciously and be their world's worst enemy. They'll forget all the things that were done for them! They will only see themselves as the victim, poor and pitiful them. So, why waste time with them? We must care for people, of course, but never take care of people. Invest in people who will pay dividends, who will grow, change and help others. This is synergy!

Many people struggled with Mary Magdalene's act of pouring a year's salary of perfume on Jesus' feet. Everybody got all upset because, "We could have fed the poor with that!" Jesus said something pretty interesting. He said, *"The poor you will have with you always"* (Matthew 26:11). Now wait a minute, Jesus became poor that we might be made rich, right? He became poor on the Cross of Calvary. That is the only time Jesus was ever poor, when He was on the cross. The only time He ever had sin, sickness, or disease was when He was on the cross. For three hours, He was destitute. He became poor that we might be made rich. Well that means that we might be, so let's be! He said, *"The poor you will have with you always."* Why? Because the poor make choices that keep them poor, they have a victim mentality. The poor don't believe they can or they don't want to do anything taught in this book. Victims don't want to apply these principles to their life. The system of this world has created a mentality of entitlement. An entitlement attitude says "You have to take care of me. I've made errors and mistakes in my life, but I'm not responsible for them. I've not been treated fairly; I am a victim. I can't be held accountable, that's not right! You are supposed to take care of me because I'm a victim."

Avoid these infectious, unhappy and unlucky victims. Their negative emotional states are more infectious than a disease. Our thoughts actually project an energy perimeter approximately seven feet around the body. Imagine the light in your refrigerator. Open the door of your refrigerator in a dark room. Stand by the refrigerator and see how far the light reaches. This is approximately how far focused thought energy can be measured. Subsequently, thoughts affect the environment and those within the environment. If you walk into a room where people have been arguing but are now silent, you can feel the hostile energy. It permeates the entire room. Likewise, those with negative energy will affect your mental attitude. Negative energy will drain you of your positive energy. You can feel your knees start to buckle. It's like kryptonite to Superman. It makes you want to run. My recommendation is, "Run, baby, run!"

Now this thought needs to be balanced with compassion, love and help. How do we do this? How do we put love into a situation? Is it being confrontational? Maybe. Teaching a person to fish rather than giving them a fish is far more helpful. It is more compassionate and loving to encourage, teach and help a person grow then it is to enable them.

Not everyone that goes through hard times is in the category of a victim. There are people who have been victimized. We have an entire population in America that has been victimized. Millions have lost their homes and lost their jobs. This does not mean they are trying to suck up all your energy. They may be in need, and we may be able to help them. There is a huge difference, though, between the self-enabling taker and an actual victim. Know the difference.

Jesus never allowed takers in His life, and neither should we. It is important to develop the right attitude and have discernment. Discernment is a gift God gives for this purpose.

Misfortunate people draw misfortune upon themselves. You probably know someone or have been around someone who has one crisis after another. It never stops. Now, I don't like the term unlucky, but there are people who appear plain unlucky! Forrest Gump said, "Life is like a box of chocolates. You just never know what you're going to get." This is not quite how he said it, but there are people who just keep getting into negative situations over and over and over (like attracts like). Often this is a generational pattern and flows down from generation to generation. This thought process can be broken if we truly desire to be free. Changing our thoughts will change our lives. So, what am I saying? Happy is good. Happy will benefit you. *A merry heart does good, like a medicine* (Proverbs 17:22). Spend the majority of your time with people who will produce positive energy. Be cautious and careful of those who drain you. Does this sound fair? Fair is where they sell cotton candy and Ferris wheel rides.

I am a loving person, but I believe in being direct with those who have a victim mentality. At this point in my life, those with such a mentality seldom approach me. I believe they receive my energy when they get close and go, "Whoa, don't go there; it's not going to be good!" I put out positive, help-your-self, responsible energy.

Your Thoughts?

Are there friends or acquaintances it would be best to leave behind? Who are they? _____

_____

_____

_____

How have they affected you? _____

_____

_____

_____

Who in your life is a positive influence? _____

_____

_____

_____

How do you feel when you're around them? _____

_____

_____

_____

So, who are the best people to hang with? _____

_____

_____

_____

Personal Power Principle 3
Fill Someone's Cup
Service

Develop a giving attitude, one of service to mankind. Work to provide happiness and prosperity for others and they will build with you. Jesus did this. He came to serve, not to be served. Service produces an indebtedness creating a return; you sow, you reap.

Serve from the heart with love, not with greed; this makes the difference. The world uses greed. God's plan is to use love. The world took the principle of service and used it quite effectively in a negative way and we have been caught in the web. When this power principle is used in love, meaning our hearts are set to serve others, we engage in loving, giving, serving relationships to help others in their lives.

Jesus did this consistently. He always served. He actually said in Matthew 20, *"I came to serve not be served."* Is there anywhere in the scriptures when He did not serve? He came to save and to serve all humanity. Everything He did was to make life better for others. He healed others; He gave His life for others. His teaching revealed the truths of God, and those truths were about serving. He served in love and that loving service produced the Church. If a pastor serves in love, that service produces a congregation. If a business owner operates in love, he produces a successful business. When done with the right motive, love is the most powerful tool available. Love cannot fail. Love is service, and service is love.

The English banking system is a good example of how the world has taken this principle and used it to their benefit. For centuries, the English bank has controlled a large percentage of the wealth in the world. What does this bank do for you?

Oh, they'll handle your money for you; pay your bills with your money. They will give you free checking and savings; even pay you a little bit of interest on your savings, say 0.25 percent. When you want to buy a house, you can borrow the money from them - as long as you have enough collateral, which means you really do not need to borrow the money. Doesn't it make you happy, though? They are so nice. The bank will even give you a credit card so you can buy today what you cannot afford tomorrow. You get to pay four times more for the charged item than it is worth, but you can have it today. You don't have to wait until you save up the money to pay (I will gladly pay you Tuesday for a hamburger today). We could learn something from Popeye and Wimpy (for those of you who remember Popeye and Wimpy). They create an atmosphere of prospering others, but the bank actually puts their customers in debt. They create a slave mentality. This is the type of system we live under today.

I am absolutely politically neutral here. I do, however, agree with our Founding Fathers. They set up a two-party system in our great country, a system of Republicans and Democrats. They knew the two-party system would be the best system ever known to the world. To this day, it is still the best governing system available. It has lasted longer than the system of the Greek or the Roman Empires. It lasted longer than any other system and I have no doubt it will continue to stand as the best. The Founding Fathers realized if we embraced a pure republic system, eventually we would evolve into a monarchy, get a king and have trouble. When a total autocracy or monarchy is instituted, the people have no say. If the wrong person gets into power, there is hell to pay. The Founding Fathers also knew if we were to go with a pure, one-system democracy, we might end up with a golden calf. They were all biblical people and knew what happened when Moses was up on top of the mountain with God. The Israelites voted to create their own god, a golden calf. People are not always informed about what they vote for and sometimes they just follow the crowd. The two-party system was and is a very good system.

Presently less than 1 percent of the population, mostly in England and America, control 95 percent of all of the money in the world. The amount of money controlled by this 1 percent is between150 and 200 trillion dollars. This number doesn't adequately measure the total wealth of the earth, not by any sense. Approximately 2 percent of the population live at poverty level. Complete poverty. In between complete poverty and absurdly rich is the middle class. In the middle class, we have the upper-middle class, middle-middle class and lower-middle class. The upper-middle class would probably include Trump, Gates and those types of people. We do live with a type of class-by-caste system. The middle class or I should say the rest of the world, lives on 5 percent of the wealth. Now don't get discouraged. That amount probably equals somewhere around fifteen trillion dollars. That's what they let us play with. It is quite a bit of money. Of the fifteen trillion dollars, the baby boomers controlled thirteen trillion dollars as recently as 2006. Today, however, they control less than one trillion dollars, and America is fourteen trillion dollars in debt.

Small businesses are actually very, very important. They produce or earn 35 percent of the wealth. In the larger picture, small businesses produce somewhere around 45 percent of the gross national product. Unfortunately, they are the highest taxed segment of business. Sixty-five percent of the labor force are regular people working in factories receiving average salaries. What is fascinating about this, only about 10 percent of the 65 percent are productive enough to actually cover wages, benefits and profit for the company. In other words, they actually work their jobs, put in their time and are going nowhere. Therefore, the competition to be successful and wealthy is only against the small 10 percent.

To gain tremendous wealth is not difficult. If you become the best worker, the hardest worker; start early, quit late, but only charge for eight hours, you can work your way up the monetary ladder and prosper faster than most of the middle class population. Everybody in the upper middle class started down at the bottom. They just found keys to help propel them toward their goal. They realized it is not difficult to beat out the 10 percent.

If your mentality is to work only 40 hours a week and no more; if you are comfortable and without ambition, then you will stay in the 90 percent group. When your mentality is "I put my 40 hours in, I'm out of here. I want my paycheck on Friday," you will never prosper. Be the best at whatever you do. Be the best your company has ever had. The best out there isn't all that good so it won't be too difficult. You can be the best. Your education doesn't matter. Your background doesn't matter. Your attitude is what matters; it is what's in your head. Are you thinking, "I want to make this business successful? What can I do to make the boss proud? What can I do to bless this place?" That's the attitude that will make you successful. You will rise to the top, and your income will rise along with you. Put your boss and your company in debt to you by doing too much for them, fill their cup! All this comes down to a service mentality and a servant's heart.

Your Thoughts?

What areas of excellent service do you provide at home?

_____

_____

_____

What areas of excellent service do you provide at your business?

_____

_____

_____

Is your life about service and giving to others or is it about what you can get by serving? _____

_____

_____

What can you do to cultivate excellent service in your work?

_____

_____

_____

What can you do to cultivate excellent service in your life?

_____

_____

_____

Personal Power Principle 4
Who On Earth Are You?
Identity

Finding out who you are in Christ is critical to success. Develop your talents—you are unique and will appear larger than life when you know who you are in Christ. Jesus was always larger than life. He forged your unique identity, who you are. You were made to be larger than life.

This power principle is extremely important. I can't explain it thoroughly enough because it is something each person must experience internally to understand totally. As I said, you were created unique. Every person is unique. Just as no two snowflakes are alike, neither are any two individuals in the world alike; hence the term individual. Because we are different, the way to achieve the Power Principle I am sharing is going to be different for everyone. The way to achieve this Principle is up to you. It all happens on the inside.

If I gave you step one, two, or three, we would all end up the same person, or trying to be the same person. I think this is something too many people attempt to do, and because of this dual identity aspect, I'm not crazy about mentorships. I know that there is a lot of teaching and a lot of books written on mentoring, but I am not excited about the concept. I have people come to me and ask me to mentor them. My answer is always the same, "Hang out here, and watch what I do, but don't try to become who I am." Too often people try to be or act like someone else. They try to do exactly what the other person does and they think it will work for them.

As I travel, I see this in pastors all around the world. They try to do exactly what I'm doing, especially the churches under our covering. I say, No, no, you have your own personality and your church will have its own personality with its own type of people. There are certain things I do which could benefit, but you can't be me and you won't have my results. You are in a different location, have a different environment, and a different surrounding. Everything is different. You are you and, you must be as God made you. God has placed you. You will draw people who are like-minded. Everything starts out with you. <u>Define who you are as God made you.</u> Don't let a mentor or anyone else define you. Forge your identity. Let's contemplate the word forge for a minute. Forging is a process where metal is heated and hammered into the desired shape. Allow God to forge your life into your specific calling.

I began to understand this Power Principle when I was very young. I spent a lot of time alone, raised as an only child way out in the country. There weren't too many other children to socialize with, only the eight other students in my class at school. I really wanted to be popular. I remember reading an advertisement on the back of a comic book. It was for a book on how to win friends. So I sent away for the book, even though it cost an entire week's paper route earnings, $2.98.

When it arrived, I ravenously consumed the guidelines on how to win friends. It actually worked! I was very popular in high school and popular with people in general. All I did was follow the steps in the book. The success of these steps, however, happened through the power of manipulation rather than by the power of the heart and who I was.

When I got into ministry, I did a lot of counseling. I had this image of who I had become. I acted it out so well, I believed it was really me. Nobody else has ever deceived themselves, I know, but just bear with me. You know how we try to imitate the good qualities in certain people? I did that all the way through school. This affected my counseling process. I was able to help people with low self-esteem. I wrote out a sheet on how to develop good self-esteem. I gave people the sheet to work on for a few weeks. Then they would come back, I would pray with them regarding raising their level of self-esteem and getting rid of self-sabotaging things from their past. It worked quite well.

I was driving home one night and said to the Lord, "This is really working. How did I come up with this idea? It's a great idea!" God answered, "Because you have the same problem. That's why you can identify with it. It came out of your heart." Surprise, surprise. Well, I applied the principles to myself, confessing who I was in Christ, developing myself in Christ, saying, "I am above and not beneath, I am the head and not the tail, I am made in the likeness and the image of God." I began to confess and speak the Word aloud. Speaking these positive affirmations aloud is important.

This is the first step in reprogramming the subconscious mind. First a seed, a thought, is planted in the conscious mind. Ultimately it's to change the subconscious, the heart. When it is spoken aloud, it gains power. I also needed to remove old images from my mind and put in new images. When I put new images of who I was in Christ into my heart, I began to actualize that reality. I became who God made me to be, as opposed to who I made me. After a couple of weeks, my wife prayed with me and for me. A ton of weight lifted off my life. I had awesome, crazy new energy. I discovered who I was and I actually liked it better. I no longer had to act, I could just be me. It's a lot of work to keep up an act. But when I finally became who I was meant to be, it was wonderfully liberating and easy to be myself. Frankly, I don't care if you like me or not, this is who I am! Really, what you see is really what you get every day in every way! So I'm telling you, find yourself! You will love being you.

Don't let somebody define you or forge your identity. Find the identity which commands your attention. We talked about this in the first Power Principle. Incorporate dynamic devices into your actions. How is it done? Find the talents you have. Even if you don't think so, you have talents and abilities. When you work at it, you can develop your abilities. You may never be great at them, but you can develop them enough to cause you to stand out from the crowd. It's not just how you dress or look, but it's the confidence you exude from the inside out. Incorporate these dynamic devices into your daily life. Your personal power will be greatly enhanced and your character will be larger than life.

Draw emotions from others, laughter, tears, etc. with your unique self. It is really worth developing. I can't tell you exactly how to do it; you must find your own voice; it's inside of you. For example, I always wanted to sing, and quite frankly, I could never make a living at it, but the recording studio does a pretty good job of making me sound good. It also feels good when I sing, and this is good. Find your voice; It doesn't need to be singing. Forge your own identity!

Here is another example from my life. I was in a little Baptist church that was teaching on the poverty of God and Jesus. This just didn't ring true with me. If I was supposed to be poor in Jesus, I was better off before I got saved. My reasoning power said, "Hey, I was on my way up. I was doing pretty well. What are you saying? Do you want me to go backwards? This does not sound right." So I began to research this teaching. I invested a tremendous amount of time in discovering the wealth of God's Word. Because I chose to do one thing, search out the truth for myself, I discovered the real meaning of His message. This truth has taken me around the world for free and made me a great deal of money. It was a tool, and now it has become part of who I am. Through it I discovered I am a teacher and a preacher. I get calls from all over to come and speak. They want me to speak about Jesus not being poor, about becoming a millionaire, and about finances. That's the only reason I'm ever invited. They don't ask me to come and teach on salvation or the Holy Ghost, I am only asked to teach on finances. My identity was forged; it is who I am today. I was led by the Spirit to God's specific call for my life.

I'm not saying everybody is going to be a teacher or a preacher. If you become a speaker or a teacher, you join five percent of the world's population which stands in front of a crowd and influences them. You may think this is something you could never do. I did! In college, I was sick for five days before I did a two-minute speech. You can, however, learn to overcome. Start with something small, maybe teaching five-year-olds in a Sunday school. Do something to help you get familiar with the area you want to develop. Do something new, force yourself to stretch beyond your normal boundaries. Step outside of your box. Get an education; teach in schools. There are many different ways to begin. You can join the five percent and find wealth in any area. You can teach on health, chemistry, or anything. You just have to find the one thing which resonates with you and forges your identity.

Let's begin to define you to a degree. First of all, if you are born again, you are in Christ with all of His benefits. You are a forgiven, adopted son of the God of the universe. You are endued with power and righteousness, made in His likeness and image. You have the mind of Christ, able to do all things through His anointing. The Father, Son and the Holy Spirit inhabit you. You can be fully confident God does not make junk. Don't pretend or mimic.

Those false states are too hard to maintain and you are too valuable just the way God made you. When you believe this truth in your heart, your walk, talk, style, and identity will be so powerful. You will attract people merely by the energy you emit. So what kind of things can you do to make yourself a little larger than life?

I was invited to Apostle Fred Price's church to share about wealth. I had about twenty minutes to speak. So how did I start? I looked at all the folks and sang out; ♫ " *Oooo, I feel good!*" The band chimed in and began to play the James Brown melody, *"Like I knew that I would now. I feel nice like sugar and spice!"* ♫ The place went nuts. Why? Let's be realistic, it wasn't because I sang well. It was because I became just a little larger than life. I was being me.

An abandoned army base in Karlstadt, Germany, where Elvis once sang was rented by a pastor for church services. About 800 people were there when I came to speak. Since I hadn't mastered the German language yet, I was using an interpreter. I was introduced, came up on the stage, opened my Bible and suddenly sang out, ♫ *"Treat me like a fool, treat me mean and cruel but love me,"* ♫ an old Elvis song called *Love Me*. Even though I did not sing the song as well as Elvis and I did sing in English, the place went nuts. They knew it was Elvis' song when they heard me sing. Right then and there, I became bigger than life to this group of people. Are you getting a picture of how this works? Find out what your talent is, and then push it. I'm really not a great artist either, but when I do a painting, it makes me larger than life, and it feels good.

A word of caution, make certain the level of your self-worth rises with the level of success you achieve or your subconscious will break down and return you to a familiar, more comfortable level of success. This concept is critical to effectively defining yourself. Sadly, I suspect the past two or three generations were given very little self-worth as children. As a result, many adults are dealing with low self-esteem. Yet, you can choose to utilize tools to help move you towards high self-esteem and success. You can begin the process by changing how you think, how you speak, and working hard towards success. Take the examples of Jim Bakker, Ivana Trump or even Jimmi Hendrix. They all defined who they were and became successful. It doesn't matter what media or arena you choose to enter. In any field you desire, you can become successful. However, when success surpasses self-worth, stress occurs. There are positive and negative forms of stress. If your success has exceeded your self-worth, you will experience a negative, destructive form of stress. Then an interesting dynamic takes place.

When the success levels of Jim Bakker, Ivana Trump and Jimmi Hendrix passed their self-worth, their subconscious kicked in to solve the problem. What happened was destructive stress. All of these people experienced negative consequences of varying types. It is a fact, the subconscious runs the entire body. When stress increases, your heart beats faster, your blood pressure goes up, muscles contract and many other destructive responses occur in the physical body. The subconscious says, "This is not good. We must eliminate the stress and return to comfort." And so a scenario is almost always set up by your body, unconsciously, to sabotage your success. You don't plan it, it just happens. Jim Bakker didn't plan to sleep with his secretary. Essentially, he was a good person. He was doing good things. He was building something for the Kingdom of God. How could this happen? It doesn't matter if it is secular or Christian. This is a principle. Principles exist and operate whether we know about them or not. Gravity is a principle; it works whether you agree with it or not. Principles stand. This is how God made us and the world. Why else does the Word tell us we need to know who we are in Christ? You need to realize God did not make a mistake, or make junk when He made you. But until you believe it in your heart, your self-worth will be lower than your level of success and you will experience negative stress. Recognize the symptoms of stress in your life. You can listen to your body and identify stress. I have to be honest. I have had stress from time to time during my 25 years at Living Word Bible Church. When I started the church it was small and I was comfortable. When it began to grow, however, I began to think I couldn't handle the growth and stress came. Because I recognized what was causing the stress, I pressed into Christ and who I was in Him. I had to continually recognize the value God placed in me. I'm not talking about pride. Pride is defined as a highly inordinate opinion of one's own self importance, or superiority. God placed inside of each of us good things. The Word says we are fearfully and wonderfully made. This is not a boast; it is factual truth. My level of worth had to grow along with the level of success I was experiencing; otherwise, I would have been destroyed.

People say, "It must really be difficult running a church of 12,000 people." My answer to them is, "Well, I must be doing something wrong then because I am having a blast! I sleep so well. Nothing bothers me. I'm blessed! I even love those who hate me." When we walk in God's anointing and follow His Spirit, whatever we are doing will be easy.

Now, I am going to get spiritual for a minute. In Jeremiah 1:5-7 (NKJV) it says, *⁵Before I formed you in the womb I knew you; Before you were born I sanctified you; and I ordained you to be a prophet to the nations. ⁶And Then said I: Oh, Lord GOD! Behold, I cannot speak, for I am a youth. ⁷The LORD said to me: Do not say, I am a youth.* In other words, shut up. We're going to work on it. So there is a process in which we can become better.

Look at verse 17 in the same chapter, *"Therefore prepare yourself and arise, and speak to them all that I have commanded you."* Many things had changed in Jeremiah's life by this point. I believe when you have self-worth, your value is equal to and will continue to be equal to, your level of success. If your self-worth is not equal with your level of success and you have an abundance of money, it will destroy you. This often happens when people win the lottery. They aren't able handle the sudden influx of wealth. It destroys them, and usually they lose all their money within two years.

If you allow the Spirit of God to reveal this principle to your heart, you will become ready to obtain the abundance of wealth I believe you were made to receive. I believe by the time you finish this book you will be well on your way to achieving success.

In Jeremiah 5, verse 17 it says, *"Do not be dismayed before their faces, lest I dismay you before them. For behold, I have made you by this time or this day a fortified city, an iron pillar, and bronze wall against the whole land."*

What is a fortified city? A fortified city has everything it needs to withstand whatever might come against it. Just as simple as that! No matter what comes against you, you have everything you need inside of you right now to overcome the obstacle. Everything to problem solve, everything to understand, everything to move ahead. Whatever comes your way, you are prepared. You have what it takes to overcome in every situation.

What is an iron pillar? An iron pillar is a solid entity which does not experience stress. Massive semis and cars drive on an overpass every few seconds carrying tons of weight. You can drive on the freeway, go across an overpass and talk to the pillar that is holding up the road and say, "Pillar, how do you feel about this; isn't it a very heavy load?" And if the pillar could speak back it would say, "No, I was built for this!" It doesn't moan, groan or complain. It was built for the stress it carries. It easily sustains the weight. People ask me, "Isn't the church a heavy load?" I say, "No, God has made me an iron pillar and I can easily sustain the weight!"

What is a bronze wall? This is where a lot of people really mess up, because a bronze wall makes a good sound, ♫ *boinggg* ♫, and it is pretty, but it isn't perfect. You are not ever going to be perfect so forget about perfection. It isn't required. Only Jesus was perfect. Don't let lack of perfection stop you from doing well.

Say this, "I am not a product of my past. I am not a product of my environment. I am not the product of others' negative words. I am who God made me. I am who God called me to be. I am moving into the destiny God prepared for me. He is fulfilling me through the power of His Word."

I want to give you one more thought; if self-indulgence is stronger than self-worth or self-control, your purpose is too weak. Poverty of purpose is worse than poverty of purse. Self-indulgence is driven by low self-worth. If you can't control food in your life, you have low self- worth. So instead of working on diet, work on self-esteem, work on who you are in Christ. And when you get hold of who you are in Christ, you will have control over what you eat, what you do, and where you go. When you gain self-control, you will be on your way to success. Without self-control, success will hurt you and those around you in almost every instance.

Your Thoughts?

Who are you? _____

_____

_____

What do you want to be (Not who)? _____

_____

_____

What image(s) identifies you? _____

_____

_____

What do you possess which will make you a little larger than life?

_____

_____

_____

What steps can you take to start being who you were made to be?

_____

_____

_____

Personal Power Principle 5
Define Divine
You and God

A divine purpose is a cause with a valued reward. Sell it with reason and excitement. Delegate tasks and involve personal sacrifice for all involved.

This is an interesting thought. As I mentioned, I gained all of these Power Principles from the Word of God. We don't need the world's way; we need a better way - God's way. This is what the Power Principles are all about. Think for a few moments about what God did, the whole process of His ultimate plan. He put it together for you and I. Jesus came with a worthwhile cause, a divine purpose. He died for mankind so we could have eternal life. God said if we trust and receive Christ Jesus, we will receive all of the promises. We will have a worthwhile cause, a divine purpose. We will become beneficiaries of the promises of health, wealth, joy, peace and great favor. God wants us to walk in health, He wants us to walk in wealth, He wants us to be blessed and highly favored; no strings attached. The Father also said, "I would like you to serve in My Kingdom," and, "I would like you to give into My Kingdom" my paraphrase. He is asking us to give a sacrifice of doing. Any time we serve in the Kingdom we are giving a sacrifice of our time. If you serve as an usher, a greeter or anywhere in the church, you give a sacrifice of time to His Kingdom.

If you desire to start a business, it should be set on these same principles of service in order for it to be as successful as possible. Build a team of employees who are willing to devote themselves to your cause. This is the norm in any successful operation. It is the same whether you are constructing a new building, producing television to reach the world for Jesus, or are missionaries taking the Gospel around the world. A worthwhile cause with value and benefit coming back to those who are involved must exist. God not only gives crowns in heaven; He wants to multiply back our giving now, in this world. He desires to bless us for all we do.

This reminds me of the putter I developed. It hasn't gone anywhere yet, but I haven't given up; never become weary doing a worthwhile thing. It's a good example of a project with value and benefit. The putter can cut strokes off and improve the user's game, so it's worthwhile to a golfer who wants a better score. It has promises; there are rewards for using this putter. It is the same principle of investing (getting the putter) and gaining a return (having a better golf score).

Whatever goal you choose; it must be a worthwhile endeavor with a promise of gain for those who become involved. Would you become involved in a project if it didn't produce increase? People will gladly give themselves to be part of an endeavor when it has value and benefit, be it a business, manufacturing or sale of a product. It doesn't always take a whole lot of money to start something, either. It just takes a worthwhile cause and someone to catch the vision. When someone can see the idea, it is likely they will help for nothing until the vision develops and produces the promised return.

Here is a fascinating fact, when I teach on giving time or tithing, I am criticized. Both of these actions, giving time and tithing, are worthwhile causes with a promise of valued return. When I ask people to give time or money, it is going to be good for them. It's going to do great things in their lives; this is God's promise, not mine. So why do people get so upset about giving when it's going to be good for them? When people finally connect to the whole idea of giving, building, serving, sacrificing, working, and helping, what happens? They gain self worth, develop good relationships, and mature. Their marriages change for the better, and their childrearing skills improve. They gain entrepreneurship, accountability, responsibility, honesty, integrity, work ethics, virtue, love, kindness, goodness; the list goes on and on, all valued benefits.

Doesn't everyone want these benefits in their life? In a successful company, these attributes are gained by committed employees. They grow in a positive way when they buy into the company's vision, become part of a committed team and ac-complish things. They gain honesty and integrity. I'm certain every employer wants to employ people who have the character

traits of honesty and integrity. These employees realize it's wrong to steal even if they don't get caught. They understand it is right to be punctual even if no one knows when they arrive at work. They do what is right because they recognize when they live by worthwhile values they gain personal value.

Consider the Ten Commandments. They impart worth-while values which support a cause. The whole Bible, every story in it is about a worthwhile cause with promises. The parables and stories all give promises of a better life when we are willing to sacrifice something in order to gain something more, something better. This is the absolute secret to a successful business.

Your Thoughts

What is your vision? _____

_____

_____

_____

Can you successfully sell it? _____

_____

_____

_____

How can you sell it? _____

_____

_____

Are others committed to the project or the paycheck? _____

_____

_____

_____

How can you develop or change to improve? _____

_____

_____

_____

Personal Power Principle 6
Steam The Team
Building

Build a team to accomplish the dream. Appeal to people's self interests, never to their mercy or gratitude. What you ask them to do must also benefit them so they will become enthused about participating. Make fishermen, not fish consumers. God uses reward, fear and intrinsic motivation to achieve. So should we.

In other words, everyone should be able to gain something personally when they engage in an endeavor. We all listen to station W.I.I. FM; *What's In It For Me*? Now you remember Personal Power Principle #3, Fill Someone's Cup. Are you wondering if this is contrary? Personal Power Principle #3's aim is to put as many people as possible into your debt through service. So how does Principle #6 apply? Maybe a simple way of explaining it is the way Zig Ziglar, author, salesman, and motivational speaker says it, "Make enough other people successful, and you will become successful." Never appeal to mercy or gratitude. Appealing to mercy is begging. For example, when someone says to you, "Won't ya' help me? Won't ya' help me? Pleeeez won't ya' help me?" How does it make you feel? It really doesn't work very well. Begging may get a few people to do a few things, but the individuals who comply probably are enablers. Enablers burn out sooner or later, have difficulty accomplishing tasks, and eventually become resentful to those they are helping. If you appeal to gratitude, it will produce people who may appreciate what you have done for them to a degree, but they won't necessarily have the character or conviction to carry it to completion. Find people who have enough self-interest in what they want to do with their life to carry a project all the way to its conclusion.

I know, however, some people will 'fall off the wagon', so to speak, all along the way. They fall primarily because it takes too much work and too much time. Hmmm… Let's see, how could one spend their time more wisely? Maybe watching a football game will produce success and abundance in their life? Genesis 8:22 says as long as the earth endures, we will have something called seedtime and harvest, cold and heat, summer and winter, day and night. These are absolutes; they will never cease. Do you have this seedtime and harvest mentality? If nothing is sowed, nothing is gained. If I don't sow energy into someone else, I gain nothing. If I do nothing new or sow nothing to be successful, I end up with nothing successful. You have to sow into something in order to gain something. It is absolutely the truth. If you never sow into someone, you will never gain anything. Both Dr. Maureen, my wife, and I live our lives this way. We do not work (sow) for personal gain; we work to build the kingdom of God. This principle always produces fruit. The way to produce a harvest of fruit is to sow seeds.

Right now I am in the process of sowing information and knowledge into your life. There are some who will carry this information and gain all they possibly can. They will accomplish what they are destined to do. Are you one of them? Personally, I don't do anything without motive. I'm not haphazard. I choose to be intentional. I try to do everything with motive and purpose. I hope this book will present enough benefit to you, so you will be motivated to read it all the way to the end and reap the rewards. Whatever you do, see it to the end. Accomplish what has been predestined for you in your lifetime.

The Body of Christ has not figured out this sowing and harvest concept. They still listen to the world's system which says, "Get all you can, can all you get and sit on the can!" The world's system is "Borrow all you can, can all you borrow

42

and sit on the can." If you borrowed a $1,000 from the bank, you would feel like you have increased $1,000. But you actually would owe the bank a $1000 plus interest. Now if you went to the bank and gave back the $1000 the very same day you borrowed the money, you would still be charged interest. So actually, you don't leave the bank with a $1000, you leave with less than a $1000. You thought you had an increase, but it turns out you have less than nothing. You have a financial negative. You're in the hole.

In the world's system, if every dollar ever owed was paid back tomorrow, there would be no money. This is why God said when you sow, you can get thirty, sixty, or a hundred-fold return. In God's system, we get a positive return, not a negative one. But people don't seem to grasp this is how the Kingdom of God works. They are so tied and bound to the system of the world, they grab at a nickel and pinch the buffalo off of it. It is imperative to get out of the world's system.

Understand the power of sowing into people who want to do something. This is what I am doing now. I'm sowing into people who I believe want to do something. I am giving you this information which I know the Spirit of God can take further then I have time to explain. When we get into God's Kingdom system and quit the world's system, the wealth of the wicked will come to us, the just.

You Ask Yourself:

Do I always ask, "What's in it for me?" _____

_____

_____

_____

What am I sowing into? _____

_____

_____

_____

What harvest do I expect? _____

_____

_____

_____

What harvest do I want? _____

_____

_____

_____

Personal Power Principle 7
Looking Good
Good Cop Encourage Us

Always be the good cop; utilize others to be the bad cop. Your team should always make you look good.

My staff always makes me look good. Even if I make a mistake, they cover for me. Again, it has to do with perceptions. How the team perceives you. When I was a bad cop, I was a really bad cop. Once I lost half my staff in one day. That was a lot of people! I decided being the bad cop wasn't working for me. Now, I have people who do the hiring and the firing. You have to be able to appear neutral on issues. Watch out for opposition with your team. I am a very opinionated person so I struggle with this one probably as much as anyone. The things I don't struggle with are the following six points I am about to share with you. These are the things every individual, whoever they are or whatever they are doing, must incorporate into their life in order to be successful. Every husband, every wife, every child, and every human being has six basic needs. If you can address and satisfy these needs, every relationship you enter into will be successful. So here they are, the good cop attributes.

1.   Unconditional Love

What is unconditional love? It is love given not because of, not if, not when. It is love which expects nothing in return, not even love. It loves you beyond your weaknesses and faults. I greet everyone as though they are the most important person I have ever met. People readily receive this as unconditional love.

Sincerity, which comes from the heart, expresses love from the heart. A dog knows if you love it or not. You cannot fake that one. People also know if your words are sincere or not. This is why your words must come from the heart, not the head, so they contain sincerity. When I greet people, it is from the heart. I only spend a few seconds with each one; otherwise I wouldn't be able to get to all the people I want to greet, but it only takes an instant to be sincere and make a person feel valued.

2.   Emotional Security

Can you share intimately from the depth of your heart without fear of judgment? Are you able to listen? The smile of acceptance can give emotional security; just a sincere smile from the heart. I greet people, shake their hand, and tell them I really appreciate them coming. Why do I do that? It instantly gives people a sense of acceptance and value. They feel recognized, as if they are someone, not just anyone. It does not matter who you are, you are recognizing them as a human person, acknowledging their worth. It is a powerful tool helping people feel acceptance and experience emotional security.

3.   Self-Esteem, Dignity and Respect

Everyone deserves dignity. Everyone should be respected. Every individual needs and deserves to realize their personal value. What can be done to elevate self-esteem? I use titles of distinction like sir or ma'am when I address a person. This respectfully places me beneath those I greet. With friends, I use the word friend. It reinforces their belief that they are special to me, and they are special. Words are extremely powerful tools.

They can build up or tear down. An attitude of superiority is dangerous. Jesus was no respecter of persons. Care for rich and poor equally, address everyone as a VIP, as though they were a millionaire. They just might be!

4.   Roots, Identity, Belonging to a Family

Everyone wants to belong. People join all sorts of clubs and programs in a desire to experience a sense of belonging. Maslow's hierarchy places belonging as the third most important personal value.

Using words such as, "We are family," is very powerful. It is the suggestion of saying brother or sister. Although calling someone your brother or sister has become religious, it is still an effective tool. All people want and need is to belong. They must fulfill their basic needs of food, shelter, love, and a sense of belonging before they can go on to higher levels of development and achieve the things predestined for them from the beginning of time.

Helping others feel better about themselves is a good thing. Why do I always say, "Welcome home," to our visitors without a church home? I believe "welcome home" means you are family. It brings a sense of belonging to the family to the visitors.

It helps establish and deepen roots which are essential.

5.   Accomplish and Achieve Value and Purpose

People need to be able to serve. It presents an opportunity for them to be a part of and become connected. It is significant for people to feel a sense of belonging.

There are people in the church who serve three or four hours a week as ushers, greeters, Sunday school teachers; all different positions and places, helping out. They are all part of the church family, they belong. If you have to be paid for everything that

you do, you have a wrong attitude and lack a sense of family belonging. Even Jesus said, "I came not to be served but to serve."

6. Recognition, Praise and Encouragement

Always greet others with an attitude of joy, an attitude of love,
and appreciation. Let people know how much their contribution
of time and talent means.

We have great ushers at our church. I like to publicly acknowledge
and thank them. What is that all about? It is open appreciation
and it gives them a sense of worth and personal value. It is also
an expression of love. You are recognizing what they do with
their talents and abilities.

Everybody needs recognition and a sense of value. I believe
with my whole heart that every person must give recognition,
appreciation and acknowledge value. No matter how ignorant
you might be in raising children, if you give recognition, praise
and encouragement while your children are growing up, you are
going to produce good kids, guaranteed.

Develop the Sacred 6
Become Blessed by Blessing Others

Are you the good cop or bad cop? _____

_____

_____

Why do you think that? _____

_____

_____

Can you appear neutral on issues? _____

_____

_____

Do you avoid opposition with your team? _____

_____

_____

Do you listen and steer? _____

_____

_____

Personal Power Principle 8
Greater Audacity
Overcomer

Confidence sells! Being meek destroys. Enter the cause with boldness and audacity, never doubting. Mistakes can be covered by greater audacity. People admire the bold and confident, not the weak or timid. Be open, believe in you, believe in God, and be strong.

Confidence is an interesting word. How do you develop confidence? I'm not certain it can be taught. Confidence can be encouraged, but it really has to be learned through your own effort and experience. Each one of us has our own unique baggage. It comes from the environment, input from teachers, friends, family, and sometimes from complete strangers. All sorts of things have been deposited into our heads from sources outside ourselves, consciously and unconsciously. This means there is no one perfect plan which fits all to becoming confident. I do believe, however, every person has the ability to develop confidence if they choose to do so. If you want confidence, believe you can acquire it and be willing to work hard to develop it and you will obtain it. Put yourself on the edge, risk some measure of failure in order to develop a level of confidence. Simply and decisively try something and see what happens.

Confidence isn't attitude alone. Confidence is an intangible quality which comes through the tone of voice, choice of words, the way you walk, how you stand, your dress; everything about you says something positive or negative. Confidence extends a desire to others to come and meet you, hang out with you, and be your friend – or not. The more confidence you exude, the more effective and influential you become. This is a power which produces authority. The Bible says we are to have authority and dominion. It takes confidence to properly exercise either power or authority.

Confidence sells; timidity destroys. Enter all things with boldness. So, what is boldness? Look at Jesus' life. He was bold. He boldly spoke to the higher echelon of Pharisees, calling them a pit full of snakes. I don't think He spoke all weak and whiney and said, "Oh golly, you guys are just a bunch of snakes." I think there was power and conviction in how He spoke His words. He had to be very confident about Who He was to speak so boldly to the Pharisees. Boldness comes from understanding who we are and having confidence in Christ.

Realize, however, there is a distinct difference between respectful and prideful boldness and confidence. A prideful attitude is destructive. It lifts itself up at the cost of others. A humble or respectful attitude is bold love which builds up. I attempt to be respectful whenever I greet somebody. I always say, "Hello Ma'am" or "How are you, Sir?" Why do I use these titles? It is a way of giving respect and value to others. It is a way of making sure I elevate others above myself. I think part of bold confidence has to do with respect, not pride. I never look down on others or become judgmental. Never think you are someone you're really not; don't be self- delusional. Pride is actually an attempt to cover up a lack of confidence, low self-esteem.

Jesus was bold and audacious. Paul said, talking about Christ Jesus, "I can do all things through Christ who strengthens me!" If you think about it, that is a very bold declaration. Most people say, "Yea, right," to this statement, or it just passes over them because they haven't really thought about what it means. I can do all things! Really? Yes, through Christ I can! This is what the Bible says and either the Bible is true or it is not.

Audacious boldness can also cover up a mistake. One Sunday, I got up to introduce a guest speaker. I forgot, however, about the special singer who was to perform first. The order of service had been changed and explained to me just before I went on stage. Now I appreciate the fact they believed in my ability to retain all the new information, but I had a lot of things on my mind. I forgot about the special singer. So right in the middle of the speaker introduction, I was reminded of the special singer. I stopped, looked at the audience and declared, "This is the second mistake I have made this year!" The crowd received the humor and the incident was over. You can be embarrassed or you can smooth over a mistake with humble, bold audacity. I utilize this whenever I need to because I am not perfect, no one is. This is an important concept to grasp, people are not perfect. When someone admits a mistake and continues on with bold respect and confidence, it is appreciated.

Another very important aspect of bold confidence is shown in how you respond when people greet you. If someone greets you with a pitiful, 'feel sorry for us' tone and asks, "How are you?" I say with assurance, "Oh! I'm really good; how are you?" I take control of the conversation, and I turn it to the positive. Otherwise I allow myself to be put in the defensive, victim position. I am not bragging, just giving simple principles which give power. People admire those who are bold and confident. Bold confidence grants permission. It gives you entrance to places you could not go otherwise.

Elvis was perhaps one of the best-known entertainers in history. Even though he has been dead for over twenty years, almost everyone has heard of Elvis Presley, and he is still popular. There are Elvis impersonators all over the world. Elvis, though, had little to no confidence off stage. Singing brought confidence into his demeanor, but when he talked, he was very shy. In fact, off stage, he didn't talk or say much at all. He used to stand and sing in front of a mirror for ten or fifteen minutes before he went into concert in order to boost his confidence. Check to see if you are feeling confident. Do you ever ask yourself; *Will they like me? Am I any good? Can I do it? Will they laugh?* If you say yes to or think about any of these things, your confidence could use a boost. Work on developing your confidence. It is a very powerful tool to have in your arsenal.

As I told you, all these Power Principles are from the Bible. I didn't invent them, and they are not to manipulate people. The Bible tells me I'm supposed to be like Christ. You won't find anywhere in the scriptures where Jesus lacked confidence. Everything He said or did was full of bold, audacious confidence. How many of you would braid a whip, walk into church and beat out the people who are trying to sell stuff? There were some who would have killed Him, but He wasn't afraid of them. You get a different image of Jesus when you start seeing the level of audacious, bold confidence He possessed. It takes audacious, bold confidence to say, "Be healed!"

Let's look at some of the most misunderstood scriptures in the Bible. In Matthew five we have the Beatitudes. It is just fascinating to me that an accurate translation of the Beatitudes cannot be found in any current version of the Bible. If they were translated correctly, as it was written in the original Greek, much of religion would have to change. I am going to share three verses with you from the Beatitudes and give you their proper translations. I initially studied and taught these 25 years ago. The first Beatitude is, "Blessed are the poor in spirit, for theirs is the kingdom of heaven." To break it down into the simplest form from the Greek, this is saying, blessed are those who are flexible and able to bend with the wind, strong in principle. Poor in spirit sounds like weak in spirit. So the translation has really been religiousized. It is unfortunate, particularly since these are Beatitudes, *the attitudes to be.* Next, *"Blessed are those who mourn, for they shall be comforted."* Doesn't that sound wonderful? Woe is me; I'm just suffering for Jesus in everything I do. I'm poor like Jesus, poor in spirit, poor in health, and poor in pocket. I am suffering for Jesus; life is so hard! Someday it is all going to be better, when we finally get to the sweet by and by. When this was taught to me years ago I thought, "Why on earth would anyone want to be a Christian? It was the dumbest thing I'd ever heard. I was happy right then. Why on earth would I want to get saved and be miserable?" It seemed so absurd it actually forced me to study. I couldn't believe this was accurate information. It was not the God I knew.

What does this scripture actually mean? Well, almost everybody has been hurt by someone. Jesus was actually saying blessed are those who become strengthened in times of trouble and press into Me; they will be comforted. In other words, in times of trouble, we are to seek God, not run away from the church or run away from the problem. It is the perfect environment in which to grow. As a result of that growth, we will be comforted, restored, lifted up. If we run away from our problems, we will not be comforted, restored, or lifted up. Instead we will be distressed, confused, and stifled.

The last Beatitude we are going to look at is "Blessed are the meek." What does the word meek bring to your mind? Well, probably thoughts of timid, mild-mannered Clark Kent, alias Superman. Blessed are the meek for they shall inherit the earth. I read that and thought "There isn't any meek in this whole world who are going to inherit anything worthwhile!" I was a rather inquisitive, rambunctious young Christian. So I studied for myself to find out what it meant. It actually means blessed are the flexible, the reed that is able to bend with the wind will live to stand straight another day. It goes deep into areas of forgiveness, acceptance, and becoming more. These individuals will inherit the earth. You begin to see what Jesus was actually saying when the Greek is translated accurately.

This message was Jesus training Leadership 101, the first teaching He ever did with His disciples and followers. How important do you suppose this teaching might be? It was the first thing God said through the Word which became flesh. It seems to me we ought to have an accurate translation because it is so very important. You can see this verse is meant to lead us into confidence and strength, not timidity or meekness. I believe with my whole heart, we must get hold of the mentality of bold confidence. How? As I said, I can't tell you exactly how to do it, each of us has different baggage to unpack. Bold confidence is something you gain through your own effort and experience. You can start by practicing in front of a mirror, teaching at children's church, getting in front of people to teach, share or talk. Go through the stress and fear of the entire experience. Don't stop in the middle, keep going until you get to the other side where you will be able to influence people. Gain a sense of bold confidence by discovering who you are and what you like about yourself. It will show in your body language, in your voice and choice of words.

In Power Principle #1 we talked about creating a power image through your walk, your talk, and how you dress, about being intentional. We are now just adding the quality of bold confidence. The meek and the weak will probably accomplish little or nothing. Everything I am teaching requires doing. It is all about growth and change. Without change there can be no growth. **Dale Carnegie said**, *"Inaction breeds doubt and fear. Action breeds confidence and courage. If you want to conquer fear, do not sit home and think about it. Go out and get busy."*

I haven't always been confident. I already shared with you in Speech 101 I was sick for a week before I had to speak for two minutes. The first time I did television, I had a fear of going in front of the camera. There are many things to go through before becoming confident, but once you are there, you will agree it was worth the journey. I believe the top five percent of the world boldly and confidently communicates effectively. You can be in that five percent!

Your Thoughts

Do you believe you are self-confident? _____

_____

_____

Why? _____

_____

_____

Think of a time when you acted boldly? _____

_____

_____

What were the results? _____

_____

_____

How did it make you feel? _____

_____

_____

Focus on that vision and emotion!
Strive to repeat those results!

Personal Power Principle 9
The Easy Way

Make your accomplishments appear effortless and easy. Never let the audience see you bleed. Act as though you can do much more. Appear energetic and strong in everything.

Never allow others to see you bleed. Remember, blood attracts sharks. Jesus did not allow Himself to be victimized. Many times people tried to kill Him, but He walked right past them and went effortlessly on His way. Even to the cross, He did not make a sound. As a Lamb led to the slaughter, He went without a word. No Protest, no whining, no crying, victoriously He went to the cross. There is so much to learn from His example. The world, however, is doing its best to try to turn everyone into victims. It starts on a one-to-one basis, people trying to steal power and place themselves in a superior position. It doesn't stop there, however, it has infiltrated all the way into social and political agendas.

Government policies, Social Security, and welfare programs are some of the systems designed to trap struggling people. They are purposely structured to hold participants in the systems which erroneously tout themselves as 'helping'. The system is set up in a way which actually prevents participants from working their way out. If you listen, you can even hear the cry of victimization from some television evangelists, "Won't ya' help me, won't ya' help me?" They set themselves up in a situation which lacks power. They work from a guilt-manipulation position, "I'm a Godly man, so you should help me." They act like victims and make those who help them victims.

So how can we have power in our lives? We can make our efforts seem easy and effortless. Never let the audience see you bleed. In ancient times, the Romans and the Spartans wore red so if they were injured, the blood did not show. Their enemy did not know when they were hurt or wounded. Don't allow your enemy to see you as weak, hurt, or in a victim position. Keep your mind strong; for our thoughts create our reality. If our enemy sees us as weak, we may begin to see ourselves in the same manner and undermine our own position. As a man thinks in his heart, so he becomes.

This Power Principle is vital and close to where I live in many circumstances. People have come up to me in an attempt to steal my power by saying, "Boy, all those services must tire you out huh?" or, "Boy, putting up with all those people must be pretty rough." Sometimes they say, "A big church must be really hard, dealing with all those people. They are probably difficult aren't they? And the weight of the all the finances on your shoulders. How are you holding up, Pastor?"

It is amusing when people start talking like this because I can perceive where they are coming from. They are attempting to place themselves in the stronger position and put me in a submissive role. They want to elevate themselves and steal power from me. Their desire is to remove me from a strong position and take away my authority.

It would be the same if I walked up to someone and said, "How are you? You don't look too good. Are you okay?" What happened during that exchange? Those words placed seeds of doubt into the receiver. They were intended to elevate the speaker and place the other person in the victim role. This principle can change who has the power. When people try this on me, I just turn it back on them. I respond with something like, "I'm awesome! How are you? You okay, anything I can do for you? How can I help you?" I do not buy into the victim role. I make a choice not to give up my power. This vie for power can occur in any area of life. You can chose to remain in a position of power and maintain authority. Don't allow others to make you feel smaller so they can feel bigger.

There is a caveat with this, however; please be careful how you use this Power Principle. There is always a balance. Keeping everyone on the same level is always the best way to proceed. I don't try to elevate myself so I can be superior. I only use this technique when I am put in a position where it is necessary. I don't want to walk around acting superior, and there is certainly nothing wrong with asking, "How are you doing?" It is totally okay to inquire about someone's health or circumstances. It is by the tone of voice and the body language of their approach which tells you when someone is trying to put you into a place of submission.

Reading a person accurately and being able to discern their intentions is an important skill. Listen not only to the words they speak, but also listen to the tone of their voice and observe their body language. Listen for the meaning behind their words and actions.

Time for a little levity. A guy went to his usual barber for a haircut. While the barber was cutting his hair, the guy told him he was going to visit Rome and hoped he might have the opportunity to meet the Pope. He added meeting the Pope would be one of the greatest highlights of his life. The barber retorted Rome was a dirty city, the people were unkind and unfriendly. He ended his snide remarks with, "And there is little to no chance whatsoever of you meeting the Pope."

The man left undaunted and returned four weeks later for another haircut. The barber inquired, "Did you get to Rome? How was it?" The man replied, "I did go! Rome was beautiful and clean, and the people were fabulously friendly! I had an absolutely wonderful time." "Did you see the Pope?" asked the barber. "Yes, I got to see the Pope and even kiss his ring. But the strangest thing happened, when I bent down to kiss his ring, the Pope asked me, "Where did you get such a terrible haircut?" This man took his authority back from the cynical barber.

This Power Principle is one to be aware and conscious of during everyday life. There are no special places or circumstances where people try to usurp your authority. Sometimes people do it without giving it a thought. A clerk may say, "No you can't return that," just elevate a little above and say, "Yes, actually I believe I can return this. Let's talk to your supervisor and find out." What happened during that exchange? Power and authority were retrieved from the clerk and given back. This is a tool which can be employed to help you maintain your personal power in most every circumstance. It is not a technique, however, to manipulate others, but a tool to help empower you.

I believe Jesus regularly operated on this basis. When the Pharisees said, "You did this; what You said was heresy; or You can't teach that...," they were trying to undermine His authority and His position. He elevated above them and maintained His power when He called them a pit of snakes and vipers! He didn't respond, "Oh, gee I'm sorry; I didn't mean to offend you." Take a look at the Word and see for yourself. He never let anyone take His power without His permission. He always escalated just enough to maintain His power and authority. The Bible says God gave us, through Christ Jesus, dominion and authority. The problem is we don't use the dominion and authority given to us as we could.

I have never taught any further than the ninth Power Principle. Why? Because the ninth indicates to never share the secrets of the other Power Principles for they could be used against me. I am going to follow my role model, Jesus, and share them anyway. It is always best to keep everyone on the same level. Remember that!

Your Thoughts?

Have you ever played the victim role? _____

_____

_____

_____

How did it happen? _____

_____

_____

_____

Do you complain about the weight of life? _____

_____

_____

_____

What can you do to regain your power? _____

_____

_____

_____

Personal Power Principle 10
Royalty
I Am

Be royal in your fashion, and act like a king or queen and you will be treated like one. Appearing vulgar and common will do you no good, only bring you disrespect. Respect yourself and inspire the same sentiment in others. Except no less than the best. You deserve to be treated well; you are the heir of the King.

This definitely wraps itself around Power Principle #1 because it touches on how we dress, how we walk, how we talk, how we act and so on. This Power Principle, however, takes it a bit deeper. We talked about bold confidence in Power Principle eight, but this Principle is about our internal attitude. Our attitude which is founded on the belief systems we hold in our heart, our B.S. In other words, what we believe about life, others, and ourselves will produce the attitude we have toward life, others, and ourselves. As a person thinks in his heart, so is he. What we have previously discussed, the way you talk, walk and act and your confidence level affects your attitude and is affected by your attitude. The good news is we can make a conscience decision and choose to change. It is something we can work on consistently. No one is perfect; we can all use improvement. It is a choice.

You can easily see the difference between a person who has a positive attitude and a person who has a negative attitude. People with positive attitudes build up themselves and those around them, while people who have a negative attitude will tear down and destroy. This is a simple, basic truth.

When you act royal in fashion, it is positive when it is not done with pride or aloofness. We need to be careful not to think or act as if we are better than anyone else. Jesus had an air of

63

humble confidence. He was well dressed, and He carried Himself as He was, the King. His confidence came from knowing He was the Son of God. It emanated from Him in His personal energy. We, too, are children of the most High King. Our personal energy will reflect this same attitude when we realize and become confident in what He did for us and Who He is in our lives. Our personal energy has impact. It effects all those around us wherever we go. The power of Jesus' attitude affected His environment, just as our thoughts form our attitude and have an effect on our environment. We are admonished in the Bible to guard our hearts with diligence, for out of our hearts flow the direction of our lives. We are admonished to be careful what we think.

Our thoughts develop the attitudes and the beliefs in our hearts, which in turn create the attitude and quality of our life. We do create our own reality. Create and radiate the right kind of thoughts and develop the right kind of attitude toward life, others, and yourself. When I think about how a king might carry himself, I think of the royal wedding between Prince William and Katherine. I envision how they carried themselves. I think of the subtle and quiet comments they made between themselves at the wedding. There was certainly an atmosphere and attitude of royalty at their wedding. Attitude creates atmosphere. The attitude I carry in my heart creates my atmosphere, just as your attitude creates your atmosphere.

Successful bars and restaurants know how attitude and atmosphere affect people, and they use it very effectively. A bar will play a slow, sad song and turn the lights down low to impact emotions and increase alcohol consumption. Restaurants use lighting, decor and music to entice increased food orders. All sorts of different techniques are used to trigger the desired atmosphere and attitude. Advertising works on the same premise. They use images, music, and words to evoke a particular emotion which will encourage us to buy their product.

I could do the same thing, coerce people into doing things. I believe, however, it's the Holy Spirit's job. I believe church should have an exciting, life-giving atmosphere and attitude that lifts people up. Praise and worship lift people's attitude toward heaven and helps them commune with God and His Spirit. Praise and worship affects your attitude in a positive manner.

The attitude Dr. Maureen and I have impacts and affects everyone who comes to Living Word Bible Church. And whether you know it or not, your attitude impacts people around you. Everyone you interact and talk with, you have an effect upon. You always have an effect on people, either positive or negative. It's a power, a force. Of all the Power Principles, I consider this one to be one of the most important. This one must be developed in order to have a positive impact and effect. An attitude of royalty is influential.

It is important to recognize that our attitude is connected to our core beliefs, our B.S. It creates the atmosphere which surrounds us. Attitudes have their roots in thoughts and words, and their power in actions. You can tell a person's attitude very quickly by listening to their speech, observing their actions, body language, and the look on their face. All those things have an effect. Attitudes tend to be extroverted. They are never content until they are expressed. Generally, they are expressed in words, body language, actions and expressions. Sometimes an attitude comes out slowly, covertly. Other times it comes out like a volcanic eruption. Either way, an attitude always comes out. You can try to hide it or fake it, but eventually it is going to show up.

Whatever is in your heart will come out and impact your life. Even great cons eventually expose themselves and get caught. Those people who say they love you but really want to stab you in the back will be discovered because eventually, their attitude will be revealed. A hidden negative attitude will come out and can be a very destructive force in your and other's lives. It only makes sense to choose a positive attitude so you don't destroy something or someone down the road, like maybe ourselves.

A bad attitude can destroy a marriage, a relationship, and many other things. Your attitude is your best friend or your worst enemy. It is always better to develop a right attitude. Attitude is more honest and more consistent than our words. Attitude is what draws people, attracts wealth, health, well-being, and joy to our lives or drives it (and everything else) away from us. Attitude has that kind of power. Subsequently, this is a very important Power Principle. It is always better to develop a good, happy and positive attitude. Attitude is the library of our past, the speaker of our present, and the prophet of our future.

If you hang around negative people, you can expect negative to rub off on you and affect your attitude. It may start small, but it will grow. "Well, I didn't think the praise and worship was all that good this week." At first, this attitude impacts and affects you a little bit. Then you begin to dwell on the thought. You think about it a little more and you begin to see errors and flaws the following week. You will find whatever it is you are looking to find. Then you mention your thoughts to someone else to see if they agree. You can see how this can grow and have an effect on many other people's lives. You begin to speak your negative thoughts and others are infected with negativity. So if you don't like something, keep your negative attitude to yourself. My daddy always said, "If you can't say something good, don't say anything at all!"

Your Thoughts

What would you consider vulgar dress and/or action? _____

_____

_____

_____

_____

_____

_____

_____

_____

How can you choose to have a positive attitude? _____

_____

_____

_____

_____

_____

_____

_____

_____

Personal Power Principle 11
Slow Down; You Move Too Fast

Never appear to be in a hurry. It betrays a lack of self-control. Discern the spirit and signs of the times. They can empower you. Be patient and wait for the right time. Strike while in the season of good fruit. Self-control produces character, which produces a good life.

I actually wrote this Power Principle many years ago, and it's really good! I wished I had lived all these years according to this one! And so will you, probably. You may not like this one as much, self-control has never been everyone's favorite, but with self-control comes the good life. The view and lilt of the world today is self. People feel it is their right to be entitled. Take England for example, they have free health care, an unbelievable retirement plan and a fabulous Social Security Program. Every government program is funded; fifty to sixty percent of worker's income goes to the government in order to fund all these things. But there's riots in the streets of England and people are wondering why. They are rioting against the rich because they want the rich to give them more. This is the same sentiment which is growing in America today. Don't touch my entitlement. Don't touch my money. In fact, I think I need some more so let's increase the taxes the rich pay so I can have more. It is a perpetrating cycle, all about self. I don't want to work. I want you to give me more.

My wife and I inadvertently became enablers many years ago. I was a youth pastor. A young girl caught a ride to our youth group. She was living under cardboard boxes in the desert with her mother. Maureen and I, being wonderful Christian rescue-enablers, took her into our home. She stayed for about a year.

We bought her clothes and helped her get on her feet. In those days we didn't have much money. We had two children and lived in a little bitty house. She was a good girl, not much trouble really. What was fascinating, though, was the attitude of her heart. We crowded two boys into a small 10x10 bedroom in order to give her a bedroom of her own. On Saturdays we would go to the Park and Swap. We picked up all our clothes and needs there because we didn't have much money. One afternoon we took her with us. I saw her admire some inexpensive earrings, and I volunteered to get them for her. Before the end of the day, she had asked for over a dozen pair of earrings.

When people get into an entitlement mentality, they think, "Now it's owed to me and here is somebody who can give it to me." It becomes part of their nature. Our nature is supposed to be, work and make money. Forget about retirement, we weren't designed to retire. I can't find that concept anywhere in the Bible. Moses got started at 80, and was 90 something when he had a child. They never retired.

Self-control is Spirit control. People say, "I want to be led by the Spirit." You can't be led by the Spirit as long as you are led by self, because the fruit of the Spirit is love, joy, peace, patience, gentleness, faithfulness, kindness, goodness, and self-control! You can't have any of the other eight without the last one. You can't even love without self-control. When self is under control, you actually become in-tune with the leading of the Spirit. It's not complicated. We have been given the Spirit of Self-Control. It's just that we allow self to control. The greatest deception that the enemy has brought against Christianity against Christians today is that it's all about me, myself, and I. Because America is an influencer, this has spread throughout the entire world's systems. The entitlement program is about self. The Bible is all about how I can give to others. The Bible is all about how I can serve others. How can I deal with whatever is in me so it is not about me? It's about you. Again, the Bible is all about others. Love others as you love yourself. (Mathew 22:38) Yes, you need to love yourself and you need to be blessed. There is nothing wrong with that, but our objective is to give to others.

The enemy has turned our focused toward ourselves. As a result of self-focus in America today, self has become our God and our new idol. We have bowed down to ourselves. Everything is entirely about what I am going to get. What's in it for me? A lot of people actually come to prosperity-preaching churches to find out what they can get for themselves. These people are misled and confused. We must be careful to teach that when give our tithe, it is not about reward. In reality, we are supposed to give because we love the Kingdom. If we give with a generous, cheerful heart, then it will come back to us. If it's just about the reward, the heart's wrong. God still has to bless us, and I understand that, but we need to do it with the right motivation and for the right reason. Because self is so powerful and so strong, as pastors we have to teach the reward. I believe in giving and I believe in trusting for the reward. This is not the issue. To believe in receiving the reward is correct, but to give just for the reward? It doesn't even sound right. Forty-two years with the Lord, I just give. I give because I want to build the Kingdom.

Self-control was a problem in the Garden, and I am going to teach you something here that will probably blow your mind. If you can control food, you can control anything in your life. Food has the power to kill you, save you, heal you. It has all kinds of power. You can't live without it; you have to have it. There was food in the Garden. We can go a lot of different directions because the Word is so multifaceted, but He happened to use the example of food in the Garden. Adam and Eve were made in His likeness and His image so they had the Spirit; if they had used self or Spirit control they would have eaten from the Tree of Life, not the Tree of Good and Evil. They would have been Spirit led.

I believe in order to have self-control, the first thing we need to conquer is food. We must control what we eat. If we can take authority over what we eat and how we feed our body, I believe we can conquer all things. I am not talking about cheating every once in a while. I had some cookie-dough ice cream this afternoon. It was the first time I have eaten it in my entire life; it was good! I am saying this to show I am not talking about law. If you know me at all, you know I don't have any laws. Law and grace don't mix. Food shouldn't have any form of control over you. You should be able to say yes or no to whatever it is you decide. Don't put yourself under law. You are Spirit led, you know when you have control and when you are under control. The Spirit will not lead you to over-indulgence in cookie-dough ice cream or anything else! We are to be controlled by the Word of God and His Spirit.

Sniff out the spirit of the times. Let me just take you back to 2006. The fall of 2006, I owned four properties up in Lake Tahoe. I had partners involved with me. They fought me all the way when I said we needed to sell. Fortunately, the properties were in my name so I was able to force the sale. I sold them at the absolute perfect high time. Everybody made a lot of money. I had properties in Mesa with some partners who wouldn't listen, and we all lost a whole lot of money. They didn't check the spirit of the times. We weren't in tune or connected with the times. Self controlled the actions, and what appeared to be great op-portunities, didn't turn out so good. Do you know what I am talking about, sniffing out the times? Now is a pretty decent time to invest but even now I would be cautious and careful. I really don't know where this economy is going. This economy is in the toilet. It's already been flushed. I'm sorry, but it is way beyond what we think. Will it come back? Yes, but self-control, Spirit-control is a must.

Your Thoughts?

What is the difference between react and respond? _____

_____

_____

_____

_____

Are there areas of your life which need self-control? _____

_____

_____

_____

_____

How can you become more Spirit-controlled? _____

_____

_____

_____

_____

Personal Power Principle 12
No Free Lunch

Loathe the free lunch, for what is offered for free can be dangerous. What has worth, is worth paying for. Pay your own way, you are worth the price. Be lavish and generous. Keep money circulating so it can circle back to you. Generosity is a sign and a magnet for power and wealth. Realize when you gain something, you lose something. As success is gained, time may be lost, some freedom may go by the wayside. Be wise, we all pay a cost for what we receive.

Every choice we make involves some type of cost. There are no free lunches. Anything of value costs something. It is important to understand that each and every choice costs. This is the way God created things. When you gain something, you lose something. When you lose something, you also gain something. It is reciprocity.

Mark 8:35 says, *For whoever desires to save his life will lose it, but whoever loses his life for My sake and the gospel's will save it.* He who loses his life will surely gain it, but he who saves his life will surely lose it. If I gain muscle, I lose time and gain health and lose sickness and gain work and lose time and gain money and lose family time, and the beat goes on. There are no free lunches! Everything has a price and it is worth paying for anything of value.

Serving God costs you time but you gain His blessing, not by working, but by relationship. Everything in life should be an investment, not an expense. An investment costs something, but pays dividends. Many people spend instead of invest. Spending is a cost with no returns, and the cost is constantly being depleted with no enduring gain. Always think invest, never spend.

Ephesians 5:15 -16 tells us to *Be very careful, then, how you live—not as unwise but as wise, making the most of every opportunity.* We are to be careful, and be good stewards all of our resources. Invest, not spend, for there are no free lunches. Having an investment mind-set causes life to grow better and better, especially in your job. It will pay great dividends, promotions and raises.

Investing is like sowing and reaping. If you sow a free lunch, you will reap a free lunch, but was it really free? Now you're only even. You bought a lunch and you got a lunch. If there were free lunches, it would have to be from creation, but there was not. God paid for us by giving His Son's life to buy us back from sin. It cost Him all to gain us all. If God had to pay, we all have to pay.

Stop looking for a free lunch. No one is entitled to a free lunch. It will cost someone else because someone always has to pay, and it's not God's plan for someone else to pay. We are to earn what we get. Then we are more likely to be generous with all, and good to all. These are investments. They keep things moving. Movement has and gives life. Without movement there is stagnation and death. Investing in the Kingdom of God is the best investment we can make. When we sow into the kingdom, a thirty, sixty, or hundred-fold return is possible. Therefore, sow your finances, sow your love, sow your service, and sow your life into His kingdom. It is an investment where you will gain in every area.

Your Thoughts?

Cons, obsessive compulsives, and manipulators are around every corner looking for free lunch. Can you identify them?

_____

_____

_____

_____

_____

_____

_____

How? _____

_____

_____

_____

_____

Where do you invest? _____

_____

_____

_____

Personal Power Principle 13
Loyal Doers
Loyalty

Always request, never demand. Those who receive requests, tend to become loyal; those who are forced or demanded upon, eventually become an enemy. Appeal to the heart and mind of others and what they hold dear! Jesus appealed to the heart with genuine love.

When people are encouraged, they typically become loyal. Whereas when they are coerced, they typically become enemies. I frequently see this phenomenon in businesses when I travel. I am always watching how bosses handle, approach and deal with their employees. I see the reaction when demands are made. It isn't very long before those employees become disgruntled and disloyal. By making demands instead of requests, many quality people can be lost. Just by using the word demand, a demanding tone of voice, or approaching someone in a demanding demeanor, can cause them to resent the request and the person making the request. A simple, more effective way might be to say, "Could you help, could you do this, would you do this? I'd appreciate it if you would do this." This approach can actually seduce people into doing and enjoying the things you are requesting. You are more likely to end up with a loyal employee when you treat them with respect and give requests rather than demands. The odds are greatly increased a disgruntled employee, or worse yet an enemy, will evolve when you make demands.

Now if you work with someone who is demanding in attitude, words or tone of voice, you can certainly be smart enough to overcome the negative and learn to live with it; maybe even help to change the person. Do not, however, allow yourself to be poisoned and become one of those disgruntled employees. Chose to do something in your own heart. We cannot control what happens to us, but we can always control what happens in us.

I was in my first year of college when Dr. Maureen and I became engaged. During the summer months I went to Minnesota so I could be closer to her. I rented an apartment in the same building where she lived. The first day I arrived, I was asked to do some handy work for the apartment building. They liked it so well they put me on another job. They really liked that work, too. Subsequently, I ended up working on a roofing crew in a local union. I went from earning $1.75 an hour to $4.17 an hour. Now, back in 1966, $4.17 an hour was a lot of money. My boss on the roofing crew was a tough man with no teeth, probably because he chewed and spit tobacco all day. He was a roofer who truly was meaner than a junkyard dog. He began screaming early in the morning and continued screaming until late at night. It is a wonder he didn't lose his voice. I managed, however, to adjust to who he was, his style and his personality. I did my job, didn't take his screaming personally or judge him. I was one of the few roofers who lasted the whole summer. As it turned out, he really liked me. When I left, he told his boss he wanted me back. This is an example of how you can adjust and even excel in difficult circumstances. However, you get better results when dealing with people, using seduction rather than force.

So now let's talk about this word seduce. As you know, the word seduce takes on a sexual connotation and produces all sorts of mentalities in our society today. To seduce actually means to attract, to charm, to tempt in a positive way. Remember, I got all the Power Principles right from the Bible. It's the very same principle used by Jesus. The Bible is loaded with occurrences of the seduction process. One example would be your salvation. Why did you get saved? Were you seduced by the great opportunity to change your destiny, or did you come to salvation because you were afraid of the alternative? Some people get saved by faith, some get saved through fear. All were seduced by the Word to make their decision, however it came. Seduction appeals to the heart and mind, so we should also. Talk to their hearts and what they hold dear! Jesus' approach was always an appeal to the heart.

The Bible appeals to the faith or the fear in people. People get saved because they are afraid of hell or people get saved because they desire a glorious eternal life. We are wired to move either towards the carrot or away from the stick. So salvation occurs because people desire the promises made available in the Word of God, or they get saved to avoid the alternative punishment. Obviously these are not the best reasons to get saved, but there is a seduction process involved in getting us to become part of the team to help build God's Kingdom. So if Jesus uses it, it must be an effective and powerful principle. I attempt to do exactly the same thing in anything I build. My employees love me because there are no demands. We ask, and if they chose not to comply, they are freed up to find better employment oportunities. So there is a little bit of faith and a little bit of fear involved. Certainly there must be an air of mutual respect. Employees seduced or charmed into doing should have promises and a future. For instance, when we start an employee on our staff, we always look for the possibility of advancement. We help them develop their skills and abilities. Maybe in the future they will take over another branch on a different campus. Or perhaps one day they will have their own church. People have opportunities to move up and advance in our employment. Again, this is part of the process of seduction. You want people to be able to move up, to give them opportunities to grow. We attempt to identify and utilize each person's skills and abilities to everyone's best interest.

God seduces us through the process of promises. We must always appeal to the heart. I use this method when I teach, when I preach, and I attempt to use it when receiving an offering. It's the same method used to sell a product. In order to successfully sell a product, you must seduce the buyer into realizing why they want to have the product. Show them what the product is going to do for them, how it will have value and benefit for them and why it is important to their life. Your product must have this type of appeal. Your job is to draw the buyer in by helping them realize how the product has all the components and elements they need. If you consider how an advertiser promotes a product, you will get a better understanding of this Power Principle. What are advertisers trying to do when they place a gorgeous blonde driving a sports car through the mountains? It's all a part of the process of seduction. Of course, the media has taken this into a sexual realm because sex sells. I understand this, but even without any sexual innuendos, it's still seduction. We shouldn't give the word seduction a bad name just because it is used wrong more often than it is used correctly. Did you know the word pregnant means fraught, filled, or abounding? I was pregnant with this book. Words become branded and we tend to think of them in just one context. Grasp this Power Principle and you will realize how products are sold.

God uses all sorts of incentives throughout His Word to draw us into the good things of His Kingdom. I hope you are beginning to understand how seduction has been used to draw us into the world's system and away from the Kingdom of God. This must change! As a born-again Christian we want to become prosperous. We believe and receive prosperity. Now what is prosperity? It is health, wealth, joy, peace and being highly favored. We want all of this! It is what God markets and what

He desires for us. God marketed this very concept in the first chapter of Genesis. He blessed Adam and Eve with health, wealth, joy, peace, and high favor. God also blessed Abraham. It didn't matter where Abraham went, he prospered. God blessed Isaac. He blessed Jacob. These promises are intended to seduce us and draw us into the Kingdom of God. The Body of Christ likes the sound of promises. They get excited about them on Sunday morning, but it doesn't seem to stick past Monday. The seduction of the world and its system pulls so strongly, people forget God's promises. Maybe the world markets its system better than we preach ours. I don't know. More and more I realize, though, if we really want to prosper, we have to separate ourselves from the kingdom of the world. Separate from its 'buy now- pay later' debt system. Separate ourselves from the world's belief that things will bring us joy. We must expose the lie which says when we finally get the right home, the right car, the right clothes, the right image we will like ourselves, live in peace and be highly favored by everybody. This is the seduction which draws us into the world, the lie in which we've all been caught. Instead of being led by the seduction of the Word, which can help us eliminate debt, help us to be satisfied and grateful for our home, our clothes and our self, we've allowed ourselves to be deceived by the seduction of the world. The Word will help us begin to live by debit not debt, and by cash not credit. The Word will help us eat just a little bit better, sleep a little bit sounder, have joy, peace and all of the good things from a relationship with Christ and fellowship with His body. The Word will help us start hanging out with the right people and doing the right things. I'm not talking about leaving every thing that's fun! I'm suggesting we let go of the principles of the world. I love to go to a good movie. I love to dance, and I love to do all sorts of fun things. I enjoy life!

When I got born again, the denominational church I was attending tried to teach me I couldn't have fun and God, too. I said, "I can't find that in the Bible, and I ain't buying it." So those lies didn't work on me, never have. There is not one religious bone in my body. Religion is habitual ritual, not relationship or love. I enjoy life, and I want to be happy, have fun, enjoy people and love God. Isn't that right? So let's get out of the world and get totally immersed into the principles of the Word, and be totally seduced into believing the Bible. This will actually bring us prosperity. Remember, prosperity is more than just money.

The entire Gospel, which God is trying to seduce us into, has to do with salvation, success, prosperity and redeemed time. He is trying to draw all of us to these things. As I've said, prosperity includes health, wealth, joy, peace and being highly favored. He also desires for us to have a mentality of success. Now what is success? Success is when you are happy and content. Success can be obtained at any economic level. There are people who are happy while living in a cardboard box. I've met people in Mexico, when we have gone down and ministered, who are happy and content even though they live in a house made of trash. God wants us to be happy no matter where we are or what we are doing. Your level of success is a choice, the power of your will, and how far you are willing to go. It is the same with your prosperity, your wealth, your health, joy, peace and favor. It is all subject to your will and willingness. How willing are you to drive yourself to accomplishments, to invest in yourself? Now the world has taught us to connect to things. If we get connected to and controlled by a thing, then we get connected to the worry of caring for it, of it being stolen or lost. As soon as you do this, you become a slave to the thing. It owns you, you don't own it. This is why God said in Matthew 6:33, Seek first the Kingdom of God and His righteousness. He will add things to you, but you are not to seek them before you seek Him. Most people spend their lifetimes seeking the wrong thing. In Matthew chapters 5, 6, and 7 Jesus delivered the Sermon on the Mount. What did He talk about? He instructed the people not to worry about where they were going to live, what they were going to eat or what they were going to wear. What was He saying? Worry comes when we get attached to things.

Have you ever owned a beautiful, off-the-showroom, brand new car? I don't care what you paid for it. You remember the first ding it got, right? Now you know what I am talking about, getting too connected to things. You didn't own it. The bank owned it, but that first dent! I used to tell people, when you buy a new car, get a ball peen hammer and go down to the quarter panel and whack it good and hard. Now you are over it. You don't have to worry about the thing in the parking lot anymore. Just drive the thing and be happy. I told my sons when they got their favorite car just beat it or kick it somewhere. Get over it. Otherwise it has you! You become a slave to it.

It's not about the things you have but it's about the relationships you have. Relationships bring the greatest joy in life, not things. It's about your relationship with Father God, and your relationship with people which is most important. Things can be replaced.

Your Thoughts?

What is the difference between a request and a demand? _____

_____

_____

_____

_____

_____

Do you own things or do they own you? _____

_____

_____

_____

_____

_____

What are your most valued relationships? Why? _____

_____

_____

_____

_____

_____

Personal Power Principle 14
No Better, No Worse
Confidence

Appearing better than others is always dangerous. The appearance of no faults can destroy you. Occasionally display defects and admit to harmless mistakes. The appearance of perfection may create envy, and envy can create enemies and destroy people. Appearing more human and approachable deflects envy. Only God and the dead can appear perfect.

You do not have to work at making enemies. They are easily obtained. I found this out the hard way. Appearing too perfect will create envy in some people's hearts. It is better to show harmless faults and weaknesses. I don't let people see me bleed if I am going through a hard time. I learned this from the Spartans. They didn't want their enemy to see they were wounded, so they wore red to disguise the blood. I don't want anyone to see me bleed, but on the other hand, there is nothing wrong with admitting I can't spell. Ask my personal assistant, she will tell you she has learned to read "Tomanese." It is all right to admit certain personal weaknesses, but there are some weaknesses you shouldn't expose. It is important to know the difference and to be as real as possible without showing blood. Be real and approachable, not better than everyone, but just as good as anyone.

This is a powerful statement. I learned this principle when I started hanging out with some of God's Generals like Oral Roberts, Kenneth Copeland, Kenneth Hagin, Lester Sumrall, and Fred Price. I realized I was not better or worse than any of them. Believing I was better would be prideful, but I am just as good as anyone. We are all made in God's likeness and His image. I have respect for these Generals based on their accomplishments and wisdom. They deserve respect for the good things they have done. No one, however, should intimidate you. It doesn't matter if it is the President of the United States. We are all just people. I can converse on the same level with anyone. I am no better or worse. To elevate a leader or anyone above you is wrong. Elevating leaders happens in the world and in the Body of Christ. People elevated Jimmy Bakker, Jimmy Swaggart, and Ted Haggard. Many people were hurt and some even fell away from God when the faults of these men were exposed. If you elevate someone, they have the ability to devastate you when you see their faults, and everyone has faults. If, though, you see everyone on the same plane as you and discover their faults, it may help you to see your own faults, and give you the ability to have compassion, empathy, and forgiveness because no one is perfect. If we say we have no faults, we deceive ourselves.

I believe being approachable in attitude generates power and energy for ourselves and those around us. We should always be kind, be good listeners, and caring people who maintain eye contact when speaking with someone. The eyes contain tremendous power, they transmit positive or negative energy, whether we know it or not. Hence the sayings, 'if looks could kill', or 'they smiled through their eyes.' If you can get close enough to see the pupils of someone's eyes, you may be able to tell how they feel about you. Dilated pupils indicate you have made a positive impression. They like you. If they don't care for you, their pupils will close to a pinpoint. The Bible says the eyes are the window to the soul. Add in body language and the complete story is told. Scientific studies such as Neurolinguistics, Proxemics, Haptics, and Oculesics have just discovered and confirmed what the Bible already teaches.

Judgment, hurtful words, jealousy, hateful stares, and envious thoughts produce a negative effect on the invisible which manifests in the natural. The envy of others has an effect your environment and your life. Everything we do in the natural has an effect in the supernatural and vice versa. Strive to be real. This will help prevent people from being envious. Extend a positive attitude, filled with kindness and care for others. This will build the right kind of energy around you and attract the right kind of energy to you. It is okay to be real. I think if there is anything we need more of in the world today, it is being real.

Your Thoughts?

Evaluate yourself. _____

_____

_____

_____

How do you appear to others? _____

_____

_____

Are you approachable? _____

_____

_____

_____

What attitude do you wish to exude? _____

_____

_____

_____

_____

What faults do you have? _____

_____

_____

_____

Personal Power Principle 15
Copy Cat?
Mentor By Example

Never be a copy of someone else. Shine your own light. Be yourself, not your mentor. Learn from, but never copy your mentor. Gain power by shining your own way. Being you is one of the first steps to success.

You never have to fake it if you always are yourself. If you have to pretend to be somebody else, there is a problem. However, there is nothing wrong with learning and incorporating principles of the positive into your life. Early on I was involved in several different churches with a wide variety of denominations; a Nazarene church, an Assembly of God church, and a Non-Denominational church. I served as an assistant pastor in these churches and observed how the pastor at each church did their job. I watched them make mistakes, and I watched the good things they did. I took hold of the good things, and threw out the bad. This was my mentoring internship, and I highly recommend this method of mentoring. Today when someone asks me to mentor them, I answer yes and no. If you want to be mentored by me, go to work in the church where I am, watch how I do things, and see how the church is run, but if you think I am going to sit down and mentor you personally, one-on-one, I am sorry. I don't really have the time. I would be grateful and lucky to spend that much time with my grandchildren. If you want to gain the advantages of being mentored, watch someone you admire and respect. Learn from the good and the mistakes they make. Focus on what works, and discard what doesn't. This is an effective and obtainable way to be mentored. This is what I have done during my life time.

My two sons, Pastor Scot and Pastor Jason, my wife Dr. Maureen, and I are all different. They don't try to mimic me or each other, and I don't copy them. They are their own person, they have their own style and their own personalities, and I have my own style and my own personality. I raised both my sons to be themselves. It is important for each person to remain an individual. When my boys were teenagers, I was an associate pastor. People have a tendency to have certain expectations for a pastor's family members. I told my boys, "Don't fake it when you go to church. Just be you. I don't want you to play church games. If you get in trouble, don't worry about it, just be you. Whoever you are on Monday, be that person on Sunday. I will deal with whatever consequences may occur." As a result of supporting my boys in this way, they have both grown up and developed their own individual style and personality. They do not imitate me, or my wife. They have become their own person, and this has given them the greatest potential for success.

Each of us are unique, there is no one in this whole, wide world who is exactly like you! Every person on the planet has their own unique cell structure, their own unique DNA, their own unique fingerprints. Even identical twins are unique in these ways. As unique as each one of us are, however, there is a critical step we all need to take in becoming real. It is our need to love God, love others and love our self. When we look beyond the imperfections of others, we sow grace and thus we receive grace. This is the law of sowing and reaping. Stop judging other people and they will stop judging you. Judgment always comes back to the judger, so don't be one. Instead, give what you want to receive, sow what you want to reap.

Work on the weaknesses in your life, don't try to cover them up. Personal improvement seminars generally say to focus on your strengths and don't worry about your weaknesses.

It is recommended you surround yourself with people who are strong where you are weak. I agree with this second statement, and I do surround myself with people who are strong in the areas where I am weak. This doesn't negate the fact, however, that I should and do work on strengthening the areas where I am weak. Isn't this what personal growth is all about? We change, we grow, and we become better. The Bible is full of change, from cover to cover. Renewing our minds, going from glory to glory, growing in grace. In order to perpetuate growth, we must be in a constant state of change, because without change there is no growth. When we work on the weaknesses in our life, I believe we activate the God gene which is within us. We were made in His likeness and His image. He breathed the breath of life into us, He breathed His soul into ours. Even though this pile of dirt, our body, will turn back into dust, the soul and the spirit live forever. God's DNA, His genes, are released within us in direct proportion to our personal transformation which causes us to grow into who we were made to be, our true, unique self. This doesn't mean we should start hunting for weaknesses and become preoccupied with sin consciousness. This is not at all what I am saying. When we discover a weakness in our life, we can begin to work on and develop it into a strength. When we begin to work on changing a weakness into a strength, we release the power of God in us to aid us in the process of change. When you know the truth, the truth will set you free. When you acknowledge a weakness, the energy and power of God is released to help in changing that weakness to a strength. There is an old saying, when the student is ready, the teacher appears. We will notice the weakness in our self when we are ready to work on it. You will become strong where you were once weak.

Your Thoughts?

What have you learned from mentors you have made your own?

_____

_____

_____

_____

_____

_____

What makes you unique? _____

_____

_____

_____

_____

What weakness do you have? _____

_____

_____

_____

_____

Personal Power Principle 16
Pretty Petty
Major On The Majors

Do not bother with petty annoyances. Don't even acknowledge those problems. You only give your enemies credibility and empower negativity if you do. The more attention you give an enemy, the more their power over you grows. A small mistake is often made worse and more visible by attempts to fix it or cover it.

This Power Principle I learned through observation and practice during my years as a pastor and a leader. When you become involved in a problem or a situation where there is bad-mouthing, defamation of character, or people speaking against you and your business, it is usually because of superficial and shallow reasons. Someone feels offended, misunderstood, embarrassed and are in foolish and petty emotions. If you fight against them, however, you validate the existence of these problems, give them credibility, and increase their power. I understand this type of pettiness is on the surface. I believe most of us recognize this fact. Nevertheless, I want to delve deeper into this anomaly because I believe with my whole heart, this is a principle which applies to all areas of our life; to marriage, to relationships, to everything! We are all confronted with problems at some point in our life. We cannot control that, but we can control how we react to those problems. As the saying goes, we can't control what happens to us, but we can control what happens in us. We have a choice of what kind of energy we produce and radiate; positive or negative. Energy is always released through our emotions. The emotion might be love, anger, hope, rage, compassion, or hate. It doesn't matter what the emotion is, all the energy we project is then reflected back to us, be it positive or negative. So you see, we really do create our own reality.

According to the science of quantum physics, we are all part of a vast, invisible field of energy. This field of energy responds to our thoughts and feelings. We project energy whenever we think or feel. It may be invisible, but it exists and has an effect on the natural and the supernatural. As I stated earlier, have you ever walked into a room where people are angry or where an argument has just taken place? You can feel the tension in the room. Maybe you have heard it said, "You could cut the tension with a knife?" Or perhaps you have walked into a room where a marriage proposal has just taken place? You wonder what's up because you can feel the positive energy being radiated by those in the room.

So we know energy is real. Scientists tell us the brain is made up of cells, those cells are made of molecules, molecules are made up of atoms and atoms are made of subatomic particles which are primarily energy. We are, and we emit, energy. It flows out of us whether we want to admit it or not. If you chose to stick your head in the sand and ignore science, okay, but it doesn't change the truth. If we become offended, take on a negative attitude, or buy into a problem, we literally empower and increase the magnitude of the offense, attitude or problem and make it worse by feeding into its negative energy. It is easy to tell if there has been a disagreement between people and whether or not it is escalating. And why does it escalate? Because both parties are focusing on the negative, consequently negative energy is increasing and magnifying, not dissipating or extinguishing the problem. A situation can easily escalate from being a simple argument into being a screaming rage match when we focus on the negative. If I have a problem with someone and I begin to dwell on it, I lend credibility to it. If I invest my time trying to solve the problem, I give greater energy into the problem and make it more instead of less. Subsequently, the problem doesn't get fixed, it only gets worse. This is why in any relationship, especially the relationship between a husband and a wife, if one person will interject a positive word or a positive thought in the midst of an argument, they can turn the entire situation around. Positive has the greatest power; the smallest light overcomes the deepest darkness. You must have light to see your way, and light is ignited by positive energy. In order for positive energy to complete its cycle, we must be grounded. Just like a car battery needs to be grounded to produce power, we also need to be grounded to allow energy to flow through us. There are many scientific studies confirming our bodies are healthier and our minds are happier when our body is grounded to the earth. It just makes sense. We came from dirt; we need to be connected to terra firma to complete the cycle of energy flow. Negative energy flows into positive energy, is then converted to positive energy and released through grounding. If you take a closer look, you'll discover negative energy doesn't exist, only positive energy. I have taught this many times; cold doesn't exist, it is merely the absence of heat. Heat moves towards what we call cold, but cold is actually the absence of energy. In the same manner, darkness does not exist. It is merely the absence of light. In the beginning God created by saying, "Let there be light." The text states darkness was, so if darkness was, God didn't create darkness. It was a condition of being without light, without God. The darkness was absorbed and dispelled by the light. In this same way, negative energy doesn't exist. It is merely the absence of positive energy.

You can impact and do greater change to an individual by investing positive energy, especially if they are sending out negative energy. This is why the Bible says when you pray for your enemies, you heap hot coals upon their head. Kill them with kindness. This is a good word. Jesus said pray, for your enemy and those who despitefully use you. Why did He say that? Maybe because it sounded so nice? Perhaps, but there is real power behind loving your enemies. It actually can make a person quite miserable when you press the power of positive back against their negative. Sending positive energy toward an enemy has the power to change them and what's happening in their lives. They might actually deal with their issues and become a better person if positive energy is sent their way. Whereas staying in negative energy only produces more negative energy. This in turn escalates the situation and causes it to become worse and worse. The power of the blessing is the power of the positive which goes forth and has the ability to change the direction in which a person is going. To agree with, to fight with, to argue with negativity, is just plain, petty foolishness. All it does is make matters worse. As I said, I believe this principle is powerful and affects every relationship and every area in our lives.

So understand the power of personal energy, the power of thinking and the power of using positive words. It is important and impactful. Positive words, thoughts, and actions create positive energy. It flows out from us, and then back into us, and builds the positive in our life as well as others' lives. The power of positive energy has been discussed for a long time, but for whatever reason, most people don't seem to understand it. Maybe because it is shrouded by confusing labels such as quantum physics or compared to the movement of *anodes* and *cathodes*. But perhaps if we look at this phenomenon in a practical, everyday situation, it might be easier to understand.

If you go into a job interview expecting not to get the job, most likely you won't get it. Henry Ford put it this way, "Think you can or think you can't, either way you are right." When you go in expecting to get the job, your mind-set is giving off the right energy. You impact and affect the person who is evaluating you with the energy you produce, positive or negative. It doesn't matter what the situation, this principle is at work. When I go into a store, I expect to be able to exchange an item whether I have a receipt or not and I do. In Power Principle One, Walking, Talking, Living Soul, I talked about how to dress and act. These things are important because the energy produced from these actions has the power to affect you and the people with whom you're interacting.

This is, in essence, how the Word of God works in our lives when it is preached. His Words contains power. They are never spoken without producing an effect. They come from Him, so when they are spoken out loud, they produce positive energy which has the power to impact and change our soul and our world in a positive way. We are what we speak, we speak what we think. If we think upon petty annoyances, we produce and emanate negativity. If we think on positive things, we produce, attract and live in a positive environment. You choose! Live in the positive or the negative. It's your choice and your life!

Your Thoughts

Do you dwell on petty problems? _____

_____

_____

_____

_____

How can you dispel negativity? _____

_____

_____

_____

_____

_____

_____

_____

Why are positive thoughts important? _____

_____

_____

_____

_____

_____

Personal Power Principle 17
Calm, Cool, Collected
Chill Out

Anger, along with other uncontrolled emotions, can be very counterproductive. Stay calm and objective. Doing good for your enemies will heap hot coals upon their head. This puts them off balance, and brings out their weaknesses.

I believe you can control and direct any emotion, especially your anger. The Bible says, "Be ye angry and sin not". What this says to me, is I can direct my anger and turn it towards good. You can be angry and not sin, or you can be angry and sin. Not all anger is bad, it is how anger is handled and directed which makes it good or bad. If you are in a fight for life, love or light, it is certainly okay to utilize anger to accomplish your objective. For instance, when the city said they would not let us build a triple-dome shaped building, I got angry. My sons wanted to crawl under the table at City Hall, but we built that triple-dome shaped building.

If it is a fight for your life, get angry. Anger releases a stress hormone called cortisol which gives us the ability to act quickly without thought, in life threatening situations. Jesus used anger to accomplish His objective in the temple. He braided a whip and directed His anger toward running the money changers out of the temple. It clearly states in the Bible that Jesus never sinned, so Jesus was not in sin when He ran out the money changers. He was in control of His emotions, they were not in control of Him.

Be careful not to be let your emotions lead, they are in a constant state of change and therefore are unpredictable. It is kind of like picking the petals off a daisy. Did you ever do that as a kid? She loves me, she loves me not, she loves me, she loves me not. It was a random outcome. You never knew if it would turn out in your favor or not. Emotions, especially anger, must not be in control or random. When stimuli come into your brain, you decide whether to send it to the limbic area of the brain, where logical thinking occurs, or the cortex area, the emotional part of the brain. You choose. However, if there is enough of an emotional charge going on, the brain will override the logical thinking area, and send the information directly to the emotional center of the brain causing a person to react without thought or consideration of consequences. This can be a helpful response in an emergency situation. It is how a person is able to stop a moving car from running over their child, for example. But we need to control our every-day anger.

Wrong anger occurs when something external, a person, a situation or a circumstance, is allowed to control and direct our anger, emotions and actions. We can, however, stay consciously in control of and channel our anger to good. Our brain is a muscle and like any other muscle, it responds to conditioning. The more we work at controlling our emotions, the easier it becomes. We can train our brain to react, or not react, in a way we choose in any situation or circumstance. If an external stimulus brings about uncontrolled anger, it will stop the flow of light (positive energy) and we will become engulfed in darkness (negative energy). When we are in this state, we often do things we regret. When anger takes over and is in control, it becomes very difficult, if not impossible, to make rational decisions. We are bound to do or say rash, imprudent things, because we have left the light and have entered the dark. The reason people have so many accidents on the road is because they allow their emotions to take control, and then they direct their anger outward. We call this condition road rage, and it is often a contagious condition.

Rational decisions are seldom made during a road-rage episode because darkness has taken over and eliminated intelligible thought. Common sense and light has been left behind.

In Genesis, God said, "Let there be light." The word light in this passage is multi-faceted. It means enlightenment, order and reason, or the ability to reason. We lose that ability to reason as soon as we enter into the darkness of uncontrolled anger. This is why spousal abuse and murder abound in our society. When we lose control of our temper, we lose the ability to think clearly and rage takes over. Self-control is truly needed in these and other situations. Self-control is, without question, an essential quantity to a balanced life.

When you love your enemies and do good to and for them, you reflect their own energy back at them. This causes them to become immersed in their own emotions. When we do good to and for others, we increase their annoyance. Did you know that? Keep doing good to your enemy, and they will just get more and more unhappy. The Lord says, "Vengeance is Mine." In other words, you are loving them and doing good to and for them and as a result they are getting madder and madder. They are going through God's vengeance. They will suffer until they make a turnaround. By doing good to and for an individual, they receive the opportunity to change and turn from darkness. You are helping them and yourself.

Your Thoughts

How can you stay calm and objective in a difficult situation?

_____

_____

_____

_____

_____

_____

Does this put others off balance? _____

_____

_____

_____

_____

_____

What will this do for you? _____

_____

_____

_____

_____

_____

Personal Power Principle 18
Find The End Before the beginning
See, Say, Seize

Plan everything. Make certain there is a beginning and an end. Take into account all of the possible 'what ifs'. In other words, plan for the unexpected. Gently guide fortune and help define the future by thinking ahead.

This Power Principle doesn't sound like it is of vital importance, but it is. No matter where you start, you must have a destination in order to arrive. If you don't have a planned destination, it is more than likely you will end up somewhere else. If there is no known ending, you will never know if you have finished. There must be a destination and a plan to get there if you want to arrive. One of the earliest principles I learned, just about life in general, is if you want to accomplish something, you have to determine where to begin and know where it is you want to end up. Then you can prioritize the steps in-between to accomplish your specific goal. Silly things have been said to describe this principle like, "How do you eat an elephant? One bite at a time." But it is the truth. It is knowing exactly what the first step and last step should be. This makes prioritizing and organizing the steps in-between easier. In order to accomplish this, you will need to take some time to visualize and think through the entire process. Don't just start blindly on your way not knowing where you want to go. On the other hand, though, I also believe in fire, ready, aim. Taking the first step of faith often seems to cause things to fall into place as I proceed. Even in this method, though, you must know where you want to go when you take that first step.

I believe God actually thinks this way; fire, ready, aim. Many years ago, God gave me a major goal; to build a domed facility. It took twenty years to accomplish the task. It was a journey of growing into the task, learning where the steps were, prioritizing those steps and keeping them in a specific order to complete the task. I believe everything we endeavor to do; starting your own business, working at a job, building a house or just building a doghouse, we must first have an image of the completed project in our mind. If we can't 'see it' in our mind, how can we do it? It takes a mental image. Emanation, formation, creation, and action are all major concepts utilized in this process. Then there are the smaller steps in between which must be done in order to accomplish the task.

Here is a great line, "Everything is created twice." First, it is created in the imagination and then it is created in the tangible, real-life world. If you were to build a doghouse, you would first have to imagine it, figure out the details of how to build it, before you actually build it. It starts in the invisible and then comes to the visible. This is the process God uses. It is the foundation of every successful business, and every successful operation a Christian does. The world also uses this method to build a business. They imagine it, see it in their mind, and work out every detail to the end result. It's a spiritual principle which comes from God's Word. It's how He created us to function. I believe the more detailed it becomes in our mind, the more it becomes a part of us. It becomes ingrained in us until it develops beyond a vision and becomes a desire, a rising passion which demands to be done. In order to be successful in anything, we must have passion and a willingness to pay the price, whatever it takes, to see it through to the finish. The time it takes, the meditation, the fundraising, the fighting; the list goes on and on and on. You must to be willing to pay the price.

Do you play golf? Ever notice on an Arizona golf course, you are always driving into the wind. Isn't that interesting? It seems like the wind never works with you. It is like the resistance incurred when driving a car. The faster you drive, the more resistance you experience. I'm showing you a life lesson here. It takes depth of passion to succeed in any venture because you will have resistance somewhere in the process of your journey.

A lot of people try to start a business, but they don't succeed because they lack umph. You can't just try to have a triumph. Try must include umph to be successful; it really does! You can't just give it a try and say, "Well, let's see if this works," and expect to accomplish anything significant. You have to be willing to put everything on the line, to give it your all. To build my domed buildings, I put everything I owned, and many years of what I would earn, on the line in order to build them. When everything is on the line, it generates a greater desire and passion to accomplish the dream. You lay everything before the dream and you put it all on the edge. You can't be successful by putting just a little bit out there, seeing how it goes, and trying just a little bit more. If Jesus had done things that way, we would still be working for our salvation.

I was talking with some of the staff and I shared my philosophy on today's forty-hour week. I think it is the greatest enemy of the people in the nation today. It is so ingrained into our hearts that when five o'clock comes around, we stop working and believe we should go home. It doesn't matter if the job is done; it doesn't matter if the tasks you set out to do in the day have been accomplished. Compare this to the late 19th century when the average work week was more than 60 hours and they usually worked a six-day week. We've come a long way baby!

The world today has developed a total defeatist mentality. Most people have lost the passion for quality and excellence.

We should always finish the projects we start. We should never leave them hanging. It would be to our greatest advantage to eliminate the mentality of 'it's time to go home now', and instead stay and finish the job at hand. If we worked this way, it wouldn't be very long before we would be promoted. We would undoubtedly make more money, climb up the ladder of success quicker, and be running the business in no time. As a result of the world's current laissez faire work ethic being ingrained into us, we have a heart mentality of being non-finishers. We start out running, and then we begin to get slower and slower and slower. The more comfortable we get in our jobs, the slower we become. It's a terrible mentality and it bleeds into every part of our lives. Comfort and dependency are dangerous enemies. We must be extremely cautious of those two.

When you are using your imagination, visualizing, lining up everything with the Word, and living your life by the Spirit as best you can, I believe God gets very involved with the energy of what you are thinking and imagining. He is the Creator, and you are in the process of creation. He becomes involved in the creation of what is going on inside of you. You just have to believe this is going on, because this is what empowered your imagination to begin with. All power comes from Him. He details everything out to the smallest event. Certainly, we can make an error here or there, maybe even miss a foundational pillar, but He is still involved in each part of every detail. Sometimes He is so amazing we go, "Oh my gosh! Look what He planned into the program." Much more than anything we expected. So always take into account the 'what ifs'. What if we did this or what if that happened? Gently guide your fortune and help determine your future by planning ahead. When you have an idea clarified in your mind, every detail imagined, you finish the project mentally. It gives you a sense of direction, a sense of purpose and fuels your passion. Now it is just a matter of finding the steps and the right plan to get it completed in the tangible reality.

People say, "Well I don't know what my purpose is, I don't know what my direction is, I really don't know." Well maybe you need to start imagining something so God has some material to work with. Maybe you need to dream just a little bit so God can meet you at the level of your dreams. He never goes past the level of your dreams.

Most people don't do what I am talking about in this chapter; this is why I am teaching this principle. You may have not done it this way before, but if you want to change where you are at, it might be worth a shot. Remember, if you always do what you've always done, you will always get what you've always got. Expecting something different to happen is the definition of insanity. Start by setting some form of goal or goals. This is what the world calls it, goal setting. However, if you want to succeed, you must have both a start and a finish. Then you can begin to determine the in-between process. What will your first step be? What happens next? What if this or that and this happens? Think it through. It's called using what He gave us, our creative brain. What are you actually doing? You are determining the future instead of letting the future determine you. You are controlling things instead of letting things control you. Most people will end up following the path in life of least resistance. What would happen to a golf ball if it was hit in this manner? We would slice the ball all day long. For those who are not golfers, a slice is a type of miss hit when the ball curves in an unplanned or undesired direction. It follows the path of the least resistance, uncontrolled by the golfer. This is how most people spend their life, being controlled by things instead of taking control. This is a very dangerous and unfulfilling way to spend your life. God sees the beginning from the end and from the end to the beginning. Let's follow His lead.

Your Thoughts

Do you plan things in your mind first? _____

_____

_____

_____

Do you see all the way to the end? _____

_____

_____

_____

Explain. _____

_____

_____

_____

How can you take the 'what ifs' into account? _____

_____

_____

_____

PRAYER OF SALVATION

Salvation does not mean following a bunch of rules to try to keep God happy. The truth is that He loves you and wants you to experience joy, health, peace and prosperity. You can only do that knowing Jesus as a Friend and Savior.

How can you be saved? It is a matter of simply believing. The Bible says: If you confess with your mouth the Lord Jesus and believe in your heart that God has raised Him from the dead, you will be saved. (Romans 10:9)

If you believe, then pray this prayer:
"Dear Father God, I ask you to forgive me of all my sins. Jesus, come into my heart, come into my life, be my Lord and Savior. In Jesus name, Amen. Jesus is Lord!"

Congratulations! You made the very best decision you have ever made or ever will make. Now you are saved. You are forgiven and you are on your way to heaven. The next step is to grow in this new relationship with God. The best way to do that is to read your Bible every day so that God can speak to you through it and get involved in a good church so that you can have support and fellowship of other believers.

We would love to hear from you!
If you received Christ as your personal Savior, we want to send you a free Bible.
E-mail us at: Thewordforwinners@gmail.com
or visit us on line at Thewordfor**win**ners.com
or drcthomasanderson.org.

MORE BOOKS BY THE ANDERSONS

Drs. C. Thomas and Maureen Anderson
A Marriage Beyond the Dream
Health God's Way

Dr. C. Thomas Anderson
Becoming a Millionaire God's Way Part 1
Becoming a Millionaire God's Way Part 2
Grace Carved in Wood
No More Sacred Cows, Grace > Religion
LOL to Life – Anecdotes and One-Liners to Get You through Your Day

Commentary of the Big 6 of Genesis, Creation God's Way
Intelligence by Design, Power of the Hebrew Alphabet
Personal Growth to Power – Jesus between the Lines (18 Power Principles)

Releasing the Blessings You Can't Contain
Will the Real America Please Stand Up?

Dr. Maureen Anderson
Releasing the Miraculous Through Fasting with Prayer
Are You Spirit Led or Emotionally Driven
Damaged DNA
Making Impossibilities Possible
Open the Door to Your Miracle (Small Paperback and Spiral Bound)

Confession of God's Word (Leather)

For more information and audio products, see our websites:
Drcthomasanderson.org
Thewordforwinners.com